ADVANCED
STAND-HUNTING
STRATEGIES

Real-World Tactics for Today's Trophy Whitetails

Cover Photo
R.E. Ilg

by
Steve Bartylla
Marshfield, Wisconsin

Photography
Steve Bartylla
Ron Sinfelt
Pat Reeve
Michael Skinner
Tom Evans
Gordon Whittington

Editor
Gordon Whittington

Copy Editor
Rita Head

Design
Brian Lindberg

Bartylla, Steve
First Edition, 2005
Third Printing
North American Whitetail
2005, Marietta, Georgia

To receive information about other products on hunting and managing white-tailed deer, please contact: North American Whitetail, P.O. Box 741, Dept. SB, Marietta, GA 30061 USA; 678/589-2000; www.NorthAmericanWhitetail.com.

First Edition
Library of Congress Cataloging-in-Publication Data
ISBN 1-892947-54-4

Acknowledgments

PEOPLE WHO BROUGHT A DREAM TO LIFE

I couldn't dedicate this book to anyone but my wife, Kathie. If she didn't believe I could single-handedly move mountains, I'd still be writing part-time. It was her unwavering faith and belief in me that forced me to become a fulltime writer. There was no way I would allow myself to fail her. Without my wife and kids, Elizabeth and Zachary, life would seem a vast, empty void.

I also must thank my mother, Bonnie. If it weren't for her lifelong unconditional support, patience, belief in me, sacrifice and countless lessons, I'd never have accomplished anything in this world.

My brother, Joe, has been not only my closest lifelong friend but also my best hunting buddy. More than a couple of items covered in this book I picked up from him. I also want to thank my cousins Joe Fiedt and George Raab, and uncle Eddie Fiedt. Each played a pivotal role in my early development as a hunter.

My cameramen, Mike Anderson and Trevor Wilson, deserve thanks as well. Not only do they perform great work with cameras and provide valuable insights while hunting, their friendship is invaluable in helping to pass the down time in the truck and while watching squirrels from the stand.

Speaking of photographic help, this book wouldn't be anywhere near as well illustrated if it weren't for my friend, Pat Reeve. Pat has taken many of the best pictures of me in here (and it isn't all that easy to take a good picture of me), as well as taught me many tricks to taking better photos myself. You'll also see his million-dollar smile in some of the shots in these pages.

In the magazine spectrum, it would be just plain wrong of me not to begin with longtime *North American Whitetail* editor Gordon Whittington, who edited this book for me. When I was breaking into outdoor writing, for more than a year I received nothing but rejection letter after rejection letter. I was dangerously close to packing it in. Then, in one glorious week, I sold two articles: one to *Bow & Arrow Hunting* , the other to Gordon. Since then, I've written more features for *North American Whitetail* and *Bow & Arrow Hunting* than for any other publications. Gordon, along with former and current *Bow & Arrow Hunting* editors Robert Torres and Joe Bell, respectively, allowed me to get noticed by others. Frankly, I owe my career to these three editors.

Another editor who has been of great help to me is Dwight Schuh at *Bowhunter*. Shortly after selling my first two pieces, I received a rejection letter from him. It seemed my piece was a bit raw for Dwight's tastes, but he offered an opportunity to call him and dissect it. During our conversation, Dwight taught me more about

Acknowledgments

writing than I had picked up in any other year's time. Since then, on a handful of other occasions he has invested his valuable time in helping me hone my skills. To say it has been appreciated would be a tremendous understatement.

Many other editors have been invaluable in one way or another. To each of the following, I say thank you for helping me feed the children and improve my art: Pat Durkin, Robert Hoague, Brian Lovett, Dan Pierce, Bob Robb, James Schlender, Dan Schmidt, Dennis Schmidt, Mike Strandlund, Jay Michael Strangis, Darren Thornberry, Paul Wait, Rich Walton and Jeff Waring.

As far as providing me with hunting opportunities, four outfitting operations have gone well above and beyond any reasonable expectations I could have had. Not only do they control the best lands I've been on, they allow me to come in, do all of my own scouting and hang my own stands. That's a special privilege I don't take lightly. All have provided me with spectacular hunting experiences, valuable information and great friendship:

Bluff Country Outfitters
Tom and Laurie Indrebo (truly part of my family)
Buffalo County, Wisconsin
www.bluffcountryoutfitters.com
608/685-3755

Bucks & Beards Outfitters
Donnie McClellan (the big brother I never had)
Northwestern Missouri
660/583-3996

PerformanceOutdoors.com
Jake & Justin Roach (close friends and all-around great guys)
West-Central Illinois and Iowa
www.performanceoutdoors.com
800/996-0477

Northern Wilderness Outfitters
Larry Golliffe (impossible not to like)
Slave Lake, Alberta
www.huntingalberta.com
866/204-8299, ex. 0644

There are so many more I could name, but the list would go on forever. So, to all of those who have helped expand my mind and career, as well as enrich my soul, thanks for everything.

Contents

Introduction

The author checks a deer trail. Portable tree stands give today's hunter much-needed flexibility in deciding where to set up. Photo courtesy of Steve Bartylla.

WHY A BOOK JUST ABOUT STAND-HUNTING?

Many years ago, when I first began writing articles, I set the goal of someday writing books. As I do with most other important things in my life, I thoroughly researched and analyzed the entire process to death, using my findings to map out the best method of accomplishing my goal and ensuring it would be successful. As many of you already familiar with my writing undoubtedly have figured out, I have a very analytical mindset.

If you don't believe me, ask my wife, Kathie. She'll gladly back me up on that one. I couldn't even venture a guess as to how many times she has asked if it's possible for me to simply enjoy something, or do I really have to analyze every trivial detail of the most inconsequential matters? (Picture a frustrated look on her face and a slightly disgusted tone of voice to get the most accurate image.) Although I could easily do a book on how analyzing chick flicks midstream is not a recommended course of action, the point is that analyzing things is simply my nature.

The only time I'm able to refrain from such analysis is when the answer is blatantly obvious to me. Even back when I first had the bright idea of doing a whitetail book, that was the case when it came to deciding on a specific topic.

Stand-hunting is by far the most heavily used, most universally successful method of hunting whitetails, and it's always my first choice as a hunter. Therefore, it only stands to reason that it would also be my first choice as subject matter.

Please don't get me wrong. I'm fully aware that other hunting methods can be highly effective. Take tracking, for example. I've had the pleasure of stalking more than one or two animals myself. Furthermore, I understand that a handful of hunters have it down to a fine science. However, the key words in that last sentence are *a handful of hunters*. Most don't have the patience, skill or drive to succeed with that tactic on a frequent basis.

Drives are a much more common method of harvesting whitetails. Frankly, when conducted in the right setting and performed properly, they can be extremely effective. However, almost every drive consists of two groups: drivers and standers. Certainly some nice bucks are taken each year by the drivers, but given a choice to be one or the other, which would you pick if your life depended on taking a buck on any given drive?

By my way of thinking, stand-hunting deer is any method that involves a hunter who is stationary for at least for a portion of the hunt. The time in which the person is stationary and hoping to bag a deer can be considered stand-hunting. If you think of it in that way, even those who employ spot-and-stalk techniques

Many hunters have been conditioned to think that deer can only be hunted from an elevated perch. But popup blinds are rewriting those rules. Photo by Steve Bartylla.

often utilize stand-hunting. Commonly, the hunter will spot a moving animal and hustle to get ahead of it, taking an impromptu stand to wait in ambush. It can even occur when tracking a deer.

Truth be told, this book will be suited far more toward the more traditional way of viewing stand-hunting. Nevertheless, some rather significant portions can be successfully applied to just about any other legal means of hunting whitetails. For example, discussions of utilizing cover to break our outline are beneficial to anyone taking shots of under 100 yards. The chapters on stand-hunting the various phases of the season will yield useful information on which factors influence deer during each phase and the best locations for intercepting their daylight movement. That information can benefit any hunting endeavor, whether stationary or mobile.

Methods Of Stand-Hunting

Before we begin exploring these topics, we should briefly cover some specifics. To begin with, what are some of the advantages of various methods of stand-hunting? Because I just alluded to the fact that traditional stands aren't a necessary element of stand-hunting, let's begin there. As stated, something as simple as resting against a tree or sitting on the ground is in effect stand-hunting.

If you're a tree-stand purist, resist the urge to raise your nose at this. Many deer are taken in this way each season, with either bows or firearms. Frankly, there are some distinct advantages to employing this tactic. First, unlike requiring a suitable tree, it can be done anywhere. That provides the ultimate in flexibility for hunting where the deer are. If you limit yourself exclusively to hunting from an elevated position, you're also limiting yourself to where you can effectively hunt.

Next, this approach provides mobility. This is beneficial in several ways. By not being tied to one spot with a stand, it's much easier to relocate from day to day, even hour to hour, if need be. Not only does this make it harder for deer to pattern us, but it also allows for minimal disturbances when relocating to where the deer are. All that's needed is to keep the wind in your face, find enough cover to break up your outline, and remain motionless when deer are looking in your direction.

If a target deer is either out of range or passes without presenting a shot, we can try to circle in front of it and cut it off again. That's how my friend Jim Hill harvested a magnificent trophy in Iowa several years back. Jim was out hanging a stand to try to take a beautiful buck he'd been seeing. Ironically, as he was hanging the stand, he saw the buck with a doe on the other side of the field. Vacating the area as quietly as he could, he formulated a game plan on the fly.

"I knew there would be a good chance that he would still be there with that doe," Jim recalls. "So, I dumped my stuff and headed out after him. It wasn't easy,

Stand-hunting doesn't always involve a stand — or even a set plan. Jim Hill is a fan of tree stands, but he climbed down when he spotted this Iowa giant tending a doe on the far side of a field. The archer sneaked close in a ditch, then hid in his impromptu "ground blind" until the buck offered him a good shot. Photo courtesy of Jim Hill.

but after belly crawling for a while, I got to the erosion ditch on the other side of the field. I figured that if he came out with the doe they'd have to circle it, and I'd have a shot.

"The problem was that I couldn't shoot through all of the burs," my friend notes. "Belly crawling through them a couple of times knocked enough down to make a shooting lane. After that, it was just a matter of keeping down in the ditch until he came out and making a good shot. The worst mistake I could have made would have been sitting in a tree that day. Sometimes, you have to get creative." You'll never convince Jim that hunting from the ground isn't an option.

Ground blinds take ground-hunting a step further toward what is thought of as traditional stand-hunting. Although blinds constructed of native vegetation, pit blinds and even some pop-ups are essentially stationary, many of today's pop-ups can be relocated easily and set up in under a minute. In addition to providing the flexibility of not requiring a suitable tree, they take it a step further yet by offering cover superior to what can often be found naturally in the woods.

I can attest to that, having taken my kids, Elizabeth and Zachary, deer hunting with me since they were 5 and 6 years old, respectively. Not only are ground blinds safer than placing them in elevated stands, but some are far more forgiving of movement and noise. The Double Bull blinds I use have black interiors and shoot-through mesh windows. That combination makes movement inside the blind almost impossible for animals to see. The benefit of that becomes quickly apparent when the first deer walks to within 10 yards of the blind as your little girl keeps tugging on your sleeve, pointing frantically at the deer she is certain only she has seen. Furthermore, as with sitting in a natural deadfall, it's very easy to abandon the blind, in an effort to cut off an unsuspecting deer, without the extra noise or telegraphing of movements that can be involved in climbing down a tree.

Tree stands are especially popular with the bowhunting crowd, for several key reasons. Photo courtesy of Steve Bartylla.

With all of that said, hunting from elevated stands is still undoubtedly the most popular method among most fanatical whitetail hunters. This is evident by the number of stand manufacturers, models and variations on the market. Strap-on/chain-on portables, climbers, slings, ladders, tripods and even stands that can transform an ATV trailer into a modified tripod exist in almost every conceivable shape, form and design. Obviously, if the demand didn't exist, companies wouldn't keep making them. Simply put, if a woman can't have too many shoes, I suppose a deer hunter can't have too many stands.

Tree stands, tripods and the like are popular because there are distinct advantages to hunting whitetails from an elevated position. First, getting off the ground typically provides superior visibility. Obviously, you're better prepared to harvest animals you see than ones that either give you the slip or surprise you at the last second. Although pop-ups have an edge, when adequate cover is present, undetected movement is more easily obtained than when hunkering in a bush.

Also, the winds are a little more forgiving when you're above the ground than when you're on it. Although it's hard to get high enough to guarantee that the breeze will keep your odor away from a deer's nose, the odds are better from a tree than at ground level. Finally, while elevated stands will never be as flexible or mobile as sitting on the ground, they're getting closer. Climbers are quieter, safer and easier to use than ever. With climbing sticks, hang-on stands and slings can now be put up in under five minutes.

For many hunters, elevated stands are the preferred stand-hunting method. However, a wise hunter keeps all options open and utilizes the one that works best for the specific situation.

Stand-Hunting Advantages

Regardless of which method is employed, the primary reason for stand-hunting is the key advantages it provides. First, hunting from a stand is simple enough for anyone to do. In its most basic form, all that's required is a vantage point that lends itself to intercepting deer movement. Of course, there's more to it than that. Still, each year many a first-time hunter takes a magnificent buck by doing nothing more than flopping his butt down on a random ridge and watching the valley below.

Stand-hunting can also be as in-depth as the hunter desires. Because of its ease, any beginner can take a stand, yet the method is intricate enough that it poses challenges for even the most seasoned hunter. If sitting on a random ridge isn't good enough, you can focus on finding concentrations of deer sign. Going a step further, you can focus on mature buck behavior and sign, positioning yourself in the most likely ambush spot to intercept him. Finally, there is the ultimate challenge of locating, patterning and harvesting a specific mature buck. One of the beauties of stand-hunting is that it can be a simple endeavor, tantalizingly complex and challenging, or anywhere in between.

Another advantage of stand-hunting is that it helps a hunter see deer before they see him. No matter how hard we try to spot deer, few of us can do it as well when moving as when stationary. While in a fixed position, we can focus more of our efforts on visually scanning for the slightest movement. In addition, we ourselves are harder for a deer to identify, even when we're sitting in the wide open, than when we're moving. As we slip through the woods, our movements make it much harder for us to see them before they see us.

The same principles apply to hearing whitetails before they hear us. While moving, we typically make far more noise than when we aren't. These noises not only tip our hand to deer and other wildlife but also make it more difficult to hear that muffled snap of a twig as an animal approaches.

Furthermore, stand-hunting allows us to better use the wind to our advantage. When moving through habitat, we have less control over where we are in relation to unseen deer. Because the most consistently successful stand-hunting approach necessitates that the hunter know the locations of deer bedding and feeding areas, along with the trails that connect them, stands can be made where the wind carries human odor away from deer activity. On the flip side, it's hard to convince a deer that it can't circle to a downwind position when you're tracking it.

Along with that, stands in funnels, near food sources and around bedding areas can be positioned so deer must either pass the stander or expose themselves to danger to get downwind of him. Finally, as stated, elevated stands can help carry the odor above a deer's nose. This is particularly true on calm mornings, when the thermal currents naturally carry our warmer odor molecules up and away from our prey.

Conclusion

When all of these factors are combined, stand-hunting routinely affords us better shot opportunities than other methods. When everything falls into place, the stand-hunter is almost absorbed into the environment, becoming an invisible, deadly predator. As the buck of a lifetime slips through the woods, I'd far rather be in a stand located along his path than anywhere else.

RON SINFELT

Starting Strong

FIND AND TAG THAT BUCK BEFORE THE LEAVES EVEN TURN.

With the whys and hows of stand-hunting out of the way, it's time to start digging deep into more advanced concepts. One of the most important is that a single stand site is seldom good from opening day through the close of deer season. This is true whether we're speaking of a relatively short firearms season or a much longer archery season.

In my home state of Wisconsin, we have a traditional nine-day gun season. A single stand site is typically not the best option even in that case. Within such a brief window, whitetail biology and prime feeding locations remain relatively constant. However, the intense hunting pressure deer typically endure during this period certainly affects their movement patterns — and thus, the best places for a hunter to sit.

Seasonal Shifts

To illustrate this, let's break down what a hunted whitetail must endure every fall. The predawn hours of the gun opener see the woods invaded with orange. In many cases, it's possible to intercept natural movement for the first few hours. Because of that, a stand overlooking a prime food source might be good. However, once the initial barrage of gunfire occurs and hunters start milling around — dragging deer, going back to camp for lunch, making deer drives, etc. — the odds of catching whitetails in a natural movement pattern grow pretty long. On the flip side, being set up on escape routes to heavy cover can be great for all of opening weekend. Another good option is picking a stand that provides for coverage of these mini-sanctuaries.

Come the Monday that is the third day of the season, most hunters are returning to work, often making it as difficult to find an orange vest as a deer. With very few hunters left to push deer, the animals' movement is at a minimum. The best bet is still the protective cover, but it's hard to get to a stand in such a place before the deer do.

Come Tuesday, in areas that enjoyed a full day's rest from hunters the deer patterns begin to return to normal. Now the protective cover and escape routes begin to lose some appeal. Instead, traditional bedding areas swiftly become good options. Except for areas with a few diehards and the occasional group of drivers, Wednesday brings an almost complete return to natural movement. By this time, escape route hunters need a break to catch deer sightings, but traditional bedding areas can be hot.

Everything changes again on Thanksgiving. Many families converge on the family farm to enjoy the traditional feast, invading the woods both before and after the meal. It's like a mini opening weekend all over again, with the same opening weekend stand placements being the best bets once more.

From Friday through the closing hour on Sunday, it's sort of a crapshoot. Intermittent pressure keeps deer patterns unpredictable. Where pressure exists, protective cover is the best bet. Private land with little or no pressure makes hunting natural movement a good bet again. The point is, to maximize your odds of harvesting a buck, you have to have several stand options, each geared towards how deer react to pressure or the lack of it.

When they apply to bowhunting, or areas that have elongated firearms seasons, whitetail biology and changes in prime food sources are the prime culprits in altering deer patterns. Over an extended period, you have testosterone levels rising/falling in bucks, estrous cycles coming/going in does, and food source availability and desirability fluctuating dynamically. To top it off, throw in the seasonal weather changes between fall and winter. All of this occurs over the course of a lengthy deer season. These factors cause changes in deer behaviors and patterns. In turn, they also should cause hunters to change their stand placement throughout the season to stay in deer.

Taking a logical progression through the season, it only makes sense to start from the beginning. With the exception of weapons, deer have most of the advantages over us. They have the ability to see much better in low light, along with the positioning of their eyes providing superior peripheral vision. Their cone-shaped ears allow them to not only better detect sound but also to pinpoint its origin with startling accuracy. When it comes to their sense of smell, we can't even begin to comprehend its power. Lastly, more than a few savvy hunters believe deer possess a sixth sense for detecting danger.

So, what does that leave us with? Aside from our weapons, we hunters have one ability with the power to level the playing field: We can apply logic and reasoning to our hunting efforts. Nowhere is that more critical than in choosing stand locations. However, to use this power, we simply must understand what the whitetails are enduring and how they are relating to their habitat.

In most of North America, early season is still a relatively peaceful time in the life of a whitetail. Food sources are usually plentiful, testosterone levels haven't risen to levels that drive bucks nuts, and breeding is still well off in the future. During this phase of the season, deer can be content leading a relatively lazy life, with their primary concerns being food, water and safety. Therefore, our stand placement should be dictated by how deer are relating to food and water, while factoring the element of safety.

Gathering Information

As with every placement option discussed in this book, scouting will be critical to our success in stand placement during this phase. For early-season success, summer scouting is a key. Summer might not be a fun time to be in the woods, because of heat, humidity, insects and even snakes, but it's valuable in determining which food sources will be hottest come early season.

One step in accomplishing this is glassing oaks. Doing so allows you to gauge the coming fall's acorn crop. An oak doesn't produce a big acorn crop each year. For that matter, some oaks don't produce any acorns at all in a given year. It takes the acorns of most members of the red oak family two years to mature. Therefore, if an individual tree produced last year, it isn't capable of producing again this season. White oaks are able to produce fruit every year, but that doesn't guarantee production. Droughts, untimely high winds, late frosts and insect infestations are just some of the problems that can cause crop failure or low rates of mast production. Glassing oaks during summer can go a long way toward pointing you to which ones should be hunted in the fall.

Various factors can affect farm crops, as well. For example, late-planted soybeans are more likely to still be in the highly desirable green state when hunting season opens. Lack of fertilizer, heavy weed infestations, too much/too little rain: All have adverse effects on crop production. A late-summer inspection shows the health and maturity state of the crop. Simply put, each plant species has a maturity state at which it's most desirable, and thriving crops have a lot more drawing power than ones struggling to produce. Summer inspection can help you peg the maturity stage and health of food sources.

Summer scouting shouldn't be limited to assessing food sources. This is also the time to gauge the buck crop for the upcoming season. For whatever reason, many otherwise predominantly nocturnal bucks don't have a problem exposing themselves in daylight at feeding areas during the summer. Employing low-impact, long-range surveillance tactics should reveal the caliber of bucks in the area. If your heart is set on a trophy, and none can be found during surveillance, it might be wise to look elsewhere.

Another benefit to observing deer is that it gives us the chance to "fingerprint" them. When a shooter buck is seen on a food source, I'll often return the next day and try to find his track. When I do, I measure its length and width, as well as note any abnormality, such as rounded tips, cracks or missing chunks in the hoof, that might be noticeable. With that documented, I can try to pinpoint his future locations from his tracks.

You can start checking the mast crop in your area long before deer season begins. Summer glassing of red oaks (left) and white oaks (right) will give you an early tip-off to their autumn acorn potential. Photo by Ron Sinfelt.

To take it further, I create "track catchers." By raking a 3-foot-long section of dirt, I can check locations I believe the fingerprinted monster could be traveling. This is an obvious benefit when you're trying to nail down the patterns of a specific buck. Creating track catchers where trails enter fields also provides a great medium for collecting tracks of animals seen when using surveillance. When constructing these quick, easy and free data collectors, cutting your odor, as if you were hunting, along with creating and checking them during midday hours, helps to ensure that you don't alert the deer to your presence.

Another potential spot for collecting tracks is around water sources. Like feeding areas, water holes are good places in which to intercept bucks early in the season; thus, locating favorite watering holes can produce killer stand locations. However, because low-impact, long-range surveillance is often impossible around water, infrared-triggered cameras are a good choice. Collecting a photo and a track is nearly as beneficial as actually seeing the animal. These units can also be utilized anywhere a track catcher can.

Creating "track catchers" is an effective way to figure out the travel pattern of a specific buck. Photo courtesy of Steve Bartylla.

Picking A Stand

With the knowledge of the caliber of bucks a property holds, what's driving deer during this phase, which food sources will likely be the hottest, and where the deer are watering, we can truly begin to select the best stands to open the season.

When selecting an early-season stand, the first thing I want is proof that a mature buck is living close by. Hopefully, that was established during late-summer observation. Next, I desire substantial evidence that the buck is using the travel route I'll be covering.

Once again, late summer's findings should have established that. If that effort hasn't, observing food sources the last week before the opener is a good

Isolated feeding areas, such as this woods-road food plot, often receive daytime use by mature bucks in early fall. Photo by Gordon Whittington.

choice. When doing this, make sure that the wind is in your favor and that an undetectable exit route exists. As you're observing, be certain to note the trail the big guy used. Then, return the next day during midday hours and prepare an opening-day stand.

Because the stand will be hunted soon, it's important to avoid creating disturbances. Showering and wearing scent-free clothing and a Scent-Lok suit, along with spraying down with Scent Killer and using Elimitrax gloves and boots, can help to ensure that odors aren't left at the site to sabotage our efforts. To further the effectiveness of our low-impact approach, the disturbances to the surroundings should be kept to a minimum. This isn't the time to be clearing elaborate shooting lanes. Instead, when preparing any site to be hunted soon, I rely on shooting windows. Furthermore, using clippers rather than a saw generates less odor and can make the difference between success and failure.

Of course, there are times when observation isn't an option. Although, if necessary, I'd strongly recommend investing in an afternoon of observation during the season, it wouldn't make much sense on a one-day hunt. If that's the case, or you just can't get yourself to sacrifice an afternoon of hunting, then you must rely solely on sign. An effective low-impact method of scouting for this phase is to walk the edge of the food source, looking for large tracks and rubs.

If mature bucks are your goal, concentrating on the quality of sign is much more critical than keying on sign quantity. I've found this to be true during every phase of the season, except breeding. Mature bucks are different from other deer. In areas of moderate or heavy hunting pressure, they don't get old by being foolish. Simply put, they place a higher premium on safety than do immature bucks and family groups of does and fawns. Because of that, they often use different bedding areas and trail systems and even may choose a more secluded food source. When setting up on an early-season buck, I'd rather cover a faint trail that's adorned with big tracks and a large rub than a beaten-down-to-the-dirt superhighway void of buck sign. Granted, you'll see more deer on the super-highway, but as obvious as it sounds, I've found that my odds of seeing a mature buck are much better in places where he actually leaves his sign.

When going in cold, I also look for remote food sources that are unique to the area. The remote aspect is rather self-explanatory. To catch daylight move-ment, you'll have to be in an area where deer feel safe. Although there are exceptions, the more secluded a food source is, the more secure deer feel feed-ing in them and the more likely they'll move during daylight hours.

Conversely, the unique aspect may not be so apparent. In regard to their taste, I believe deer are somewhat like us. My two favorite meals are steak din-ners and pepperoni pizza. However, if forced to eat them every day, I'd get awfully tired of those meals. All of a sudden, a pasta dinner would be very appealing. I believe the same can be said of deer.

To help prove this theory, let's consider the winter feeding patterns of the deer on a property I used to own. The feed I used consisted of a mixture of Antler King Trophy Deer & Elk Pellets, corn and wheat. It more than met all of the herd's nutritional needs and was vastly superior to any other option in the area. Still, as soon as the spring melt occurred, the deer stopped using the feed station. Why would they abandon such a supe-rior food source, even before the new seedlings appeared? I believe it was because they craved something — *anything* — different from what they had been eating every day for months on end. Because of that trait, desirable unique food sources can be magnets for whitetails.

When you can find a remote, unique food source, get ready for some fantastic early-season hunting. The best example of this was the results of my work in 2003. Selecting an area completely encased by woods, I created a 3-acre plot of soy-beans. In an effort to produce the only beans still green during hunt-ing season, I'd planted it very late. My hope was that the feeling of safety, combined with a unique,

In agricultural areas, a field of late-planted soybeans is frequently a real deer magnet around the opening of bow season. Photo by Ron Sinfelt.

highly desirable food source, would be irresistible to the bucks.

I wasn't disappointed. Sitting on the plot the second day of the season was one of those sits that fly by so swiftly you almost feel cheated that it didn't go on longer. Before climbing down from the tree, I had seen four 1 1/2-year-old bucks and two 2 1/2-year-old bucks and had passed on a clear shot at a perfect 140-inch 10-pointer.

The second afternoon, I watched as a Boone and Crockett 5x5 slowly fed his way across the beans. Flanked on both sides by his yearling buddies, he came dangerously close to entering my bow range. Suddenly, the group snapped their heads up and froze. After meticulously examining the woods in search of the answer to what was making the undetermined sounds, one of the young bucks decided to bolt, dragging his buddies along with him. Less than 30 seconds later, the wide 3 1/2-year-old 8-pointer emerged. Before darkness came, I'd seen nine yearlings, a 3 1/2 and one mature buck that netted B&C, for a two-afternoon total of 18 bucks sighted. A little over a week later, I filled my buck tag.

That hunt occurred on a farm I worked on for Bluff Country Outfitters. In total, that one 500-acre farm produced six wall-hangers for Tom Indrebo's clients in 2003, including the B&C 10-pointer! Although it was already a good farm, introducing secluded, unique food sources played a key role in the outfitter's success that season.

In the case of the bean plot, I set my stand right on the edge of the feeding area. I believed that the bucks would feel safe there during daylight, and I had a good exit route from the stand. With the stand positioned in the corner where the old access road entered, I had a quiet route out. If deer were close, I had to wait them out before I could leave. It could be a hassle, but it was worth it for the shot opportunities presented by bucks that entered the plot by various trails, only to feed their way within range of my stand. When either good exit routes from the food source don't exist or the bucks are arriving after dark to feed, following their trails back into the woods to the staging area is the best approach.

Conclusion

Early-season success hinges on finding areas that hold mature bucks, locating hot food sources, pinpointing the right trail and going undetected. At this time, more than any other except late season, bucks are easily patterned. For those who do their homework, that makes the first weeks of bow season a great time to arrow a mature buck.

RON SINFELT

Hunting the Lull

WHEN THE WOODS GO DEAD, SIT ON A GOOD RUB LINE.

As nice as it is to get out and enjoy the first week or two of archery season, the appeal fades swiftly. Almost with a flick of a switch, the same food sources that were teeming with bucks go dead. Even if bucks are still feeding there, they're doing so only at night.

A good example of this is the buck activity on that 3-acre patch of soybeans described in Chapter 1. Because of an ideal setting and a great low-impact access route, along with a unique yet highly desirable crop, I had four separate bachelor groups of bucks competing for it. That fall, the first week and a half of bow season was better than any I had ever experienced at that time of year.

Then, it happened: The field went as cold as a block of ice. Why? Good question. The beans were still green, no apparent changes in the area's other food sources had occurred, and deer were still oblivious to being hunted on the food plot.

In my years of having hunted whitetails in numerous states, I've noticed that same trend in each. In remote locations where deer feel safe, the first week or two (sometimes even three) offer great hunting around food sources. However, the action almost always ends abruptly. After being shut down on a food source, I've even glassed the fields of farms that don't allow any hunting and have noticed a distinctive lack of mature bucks feeding there in daylight, as well.

This sudden lull is as common for seasons that begin in September as for those that open in October. Certainly, there's always the exception; even areas that shut down can yield an occasional mature buck feeding during daylight hours. However, more often than not, you can bank on it grinding to a virtual halt.

This might be attributed to hunting pressure, acorn crops, bachelor groups disbanding, etc. But as much as any of those, I suspect the approaching rut is a key factor. Because of the incredible strain the rut puts on a mature buck, there are advantages to resting his body beforehand. It's like the calm before the storm.

Regardless of why this lull occurs, hunters who strive to stay in trophy bucks all season must adjust their tactics. By far the best way I've found of accomplishing this is to hunt stands close to where mature bucks bed. This can be a rather challenging and risky endeavor, but, if done properly, it can be productive at a time when everything else is hit-or-miss.

Characteristics Of A Big Buck's Bed

Obviously, the first step in hunting a mature buck's bedding area is finding it. Understanding the features bucks look for helps greatly in that quest.

Upon finding any significant deer sign, I always stand there for a moment and analyze why it was left in that specific location. Doing so helps me anticipate where else I might find similar evidence of that behavior. Having done that with every bed I have come across for many years now, I've been able to generate the following list of what mature bucks desire in their bedding areas: (1) the thickest cover in the area; (2) vantage points geared for seeing approaching danger from a distance; (3) locations where approaching danger can't help but make noise; (4) escape routes enabling the deer to slip to safety; and (5) positioning that takes advantage of wind direction.

From this list, we can break a mature buck's bedding area into three categories: beds that hide the animal (typically located in heavy cover); beds that offer superior visibility (open and/or elevated surroundings); and the rarer situation in which a bedding spot offers visibility and cover.

Hidden beds typically offer noises that alert the buck to approaching danger, the ability to utilize the wind and numerous escape routes — all at the cost of seeing danger from a distance. Common examples of this include swamps, clearcut regrowth, thickets, dense groves of young evergreens, brush-choked areas and standing cornfields. Unless there is a topographic rise in the middle of the cover, a deer can't see far in any one of those settings. However, anyone who's ever tried to sneak through one of them realizes it's all but impossible to do so unless conditions are perfect.

FINDING BUCK BEDS

Bucks seek security in their bedding spots. That means at least one of the following features is typically present:

1. **Thickest cover in the area**

2. **Good vantage point**

3. **Noisy to move through**

4. **Good escape route(s)**

5. **Advantageous air flow**

Clearly, deer can bed with the wind to cover their backside. As an added bonus, because of the pain of walking through these areas, humans typically stay out. Finally, when we do venture in, nearly every direction of approach offers deer ample escape routes, including doing nothing more than circling behind the intruder. This all adds up to heavy cover being a great bedding location.

With the exception of rises in the cover, the cost of superior visibility is a lack of protective cover and noisy approaches. With those exceptions, these locations offer everything else from our list. Little knobs and fingers of ridges, along with high points in overgrown fields and brushland, are prime examples. By bedding so the wind covers the backside of the ridge or high point, the deer can easily see danger approaching from the front or to either side and smell it coming from behind. To escape, all the deer must do is drop down to the side away from danger. As soon as the deer drops below the crest, it is out of harm's way.

Lastly, when significant rises occur in cover, the mature buck has it all. These spots offer the best of both worlds and are highly coveted bedding sites. Although family groups and young bucks might bed nearly anywhere, the mature buck isn't afforded that luxury. Because of hunting pressure, bucks don't get old by being stupid. If they're careless in where they bed, they're typically harvested before their third birthday. Because they cherish their life, almost every action they take other than during the rut has a built-in safety factor. Selecting bedding areas is certainly not an exception. That understanding helps to lead us to where the monarchs bed. When all else fails, think of the list and ask yourself what spots provide the best of those features. Nine times out of 10, that's where you'll find his bed.

Finding Where They Crash

With that understanding, we can now employ aerial photos and topographical (contour) maps to find likely locations. With a little practice, studying a detailed aerial photo can reveal pockets of thick cover, along with swamps, brush-choked bottoms and overgrown fields. In areas of significant topographical relief, aerial photos can even reveal points and knobs on ridges. Once we learn to read contours, topographical maps make finding the rises and knobs child's play.

Using these tools, we can make educated guesses as to where the big boys are bedding. Of course, we still need to get out there and verify it for ourselves. In some areas, maps and photos will do so well that the trained eye can find all of the best spots by using them. When that's the case, a quick foot-scouting session will be enough.

However, some settings don't yield obvious bedding areas. That's where it gets a little more challenging. That's also where those who hunt areas that receive annual snowfalls have an advantage. Getting on a set of large tracks and following them backwards reveals as much of a mature buck's life as the hunter is willing to pursue. Under these conditions, beds stick out like a sore thumb.

You'll often find the beds of mature bucks in open habitat, such as CRP fields of tall grass and/or brush. Photo by Gordon Whittington.

When employing this tactic, apply common sense. First, in the far North, deer migrate to yarding areas. In other areas that experience cold winters, deer place a higher premium on bedding sites that provide protection from the harsh elements at that time than they do in the fall. Obviously, under either of those conditions, many of the lull period's bedding areas will be abandoned.

Another consideration is that, because a buck's life revolves around food and water during the lull period, those things will have an impact on where he beds. When winter food sources are well removed from the sources depended upon in fall, the bedding areas won't be in the same locations. However, when they are relatively close, the odds are good that the beds the deer use in January will be the same ones used during the lull period. To further improve your odds, look for rubs in the general

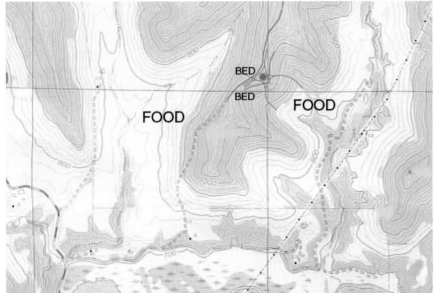

The red dot marks the stand from which the author shot a big Wisconsin 10-pointer while bowhunting with Bluff Country Outfitters. With the timbered ridge forming a steep point, the stand was set to intercept the buck as he went from either bedding spot to one of his two food sources. Steve located the beds by following the big deer's rub lines. Map courtesy of U.S. Geological Survey.

vicinity. That is yet another indication that the area was used during the fall.

The other time of year I depend on heavily for locating bucks' bedding areas is spring. Before spring green-up is a fantastic time to scout for many phases of deer season, including this one. Because all of the rubs from the previous fall are still clearly visible, this is the best time I've found to piece together rub lines that run between feeding and bedding areas.

To do this, I circle last fall's food sources, looking for rubs and trails. Upon finding either, I follow them back into the woods. Commonly, the locations where the family group's trail fades out are the places where the does and fawns sleep. When the trail breaks up, I begin searching for depressions and debris-free ovals that indicate bedding activity. If the beds range from small to large, you know you've found a family group's bedding area. This location is then logged for use during and around the rut.

Following rub lines is the best way of foot scouting to locate a mature buck's bedding area, but pulling it off can be a bit of a challenge. Most bucks just aren't considerate enough to leave evenly spaced rubs marking paths to their beds. More

By using common sense, you should be able to tell whether a buck's rub line is being hit mainly in the morning or the afternoon. Photo by Michael Skinner.

often that not, you'll find two or three here, a space with none, and then a handful more. That's why it's so beneficial that spring holds all of the previous fall's rubs and provides woods void of foliage. Those factors, combined with thorough scouting, can help us connect these lines with the maker's bed. Unlike the family group's bedding areas, the depressions and debris-free ovals should all be large. Along with the rub line, it helps to ensure that you've found where a big boy sleeps.

When playing "connect the dots," pay attention to the size of any rubs and the ferocity with which they've been attacked. As most hunters know, big rubs typically indicate big bucks. However, big bucks will often rub on smaller-diameter trees, as well. An indication of the size of the maker is the level of damage. When saplings are trashed, not just rubbed a bit, it's a good bet that a big boy did the damage.

Another point to note is the direction the rubbed side of the tree is facing. Granted, bucks often circle a tree when rubbing. However, if eight of 10 rubbed areas point toward the feeding area, it's a fairly safe bet you have located the path the buck took while returning to his bed, and you thus could assume that the rubs were worked in the mornings. Rubbed areas facing toward the bed indicate an evening route used to move toward the food.

The drawback to spring scouting is that the maker of this sign might be dead before you ever find it. However, because a mature buck places such a premium on his safety, you can bet there was a reason he chose that bedding site, used that travel corridor, and fed in that location. Assuming drastic changes to the habitat don't occur, you can bet that another buck is waiting in line to fill the void.

Hunting The Edges

Obviously, the first challenge in hunting bedding areas is finding where at least one mature buck sleeps. With that accomplished, we're well on our way. Still, there are challenges left to overcome. Somehow we need to get as close as we can to the one area in which big bucks are least tolerant of disturbances. The closer we get, the better the odds are that we'll observe daylight movement — but so are the chances of the deer busting us.

Frankly, there's no cut-and-dried answer to how close we can get to a buck's bed without blowing it. Many factors, such as wind direction, topography, visibility, the noisiness of ground cover, and the hunter's own ability to sneak through the woods, all work together to decide what this distance is. In short, the answer is dictated by the quality of existing approach routes and how cautious the hunter is.

To start out, it's better to play it a little on the safe side than to gamble. If we set up too far from the bed, we might not see the buck in daylight, but we can always adjust closer. However, if we start out too close to the bed and don't get the deer, once he's pegged us enough times, he'll vanish.

An example of finding that balance will finish off the recounting of my experiences on the Wisconsin farm discussed in Chapter 1. As you'll recall, the season began with incredible sightings on the food plot, including a very close call with a monster buck. However, keeping with seasonal trends, the spot went cold before I filled my tag. Luckily, I had anticipated that, and well before the season I'd targeted a location for hunting this lull period.

Part of the reason I selected the location for the food plot was that I knew corn would be planted above the bottom. With a 100- to 200-yard-wide strip of woods making up the sidehill, it was a pretty safe bet that deer would be bedding in the corn and dropping to the food plot to feed. Numerous sightings the first week proved that to be true.

Once the bucks started moving, it was time to sit the stand next to the corn. Because

Anticipating the lull period and setting up a stand specifically for it allowed the author to arrow this unique Wisconsin whitetail. Photo courtesy of Steve Bartylla.

the field had been in another crop the previous year, old sign wasn't available to key stand placement on. However, one corner in particular was attractive. The farm was set up like a three-step staircase. The lowest step was the bottom containing my food plot. The next step up was the cornfield, with a step above that being the neighbor's large hayfield. The woods consisted of the two sidehills, along with a larger body off to the north of the fields.

The appealing corner had a gentle finger dropping from the top step and flattening out just before reaching the corn. With sharp climbs on either side, the finger was the easiest travel route between the top two steps. Also, being on the corner, it was ideal for catching movement paralleling two sides of the standing corn. The deer could exit their cornfield bedding area and use the edge for protection as they traveled the first leg to that night's food choice. If they sensed danger, two bounds and they were back into the safety of the bedding area. Because of the combination of the natural funnel of the finger and a low-impact approach route, I was confident this stand could produce.

That's the location I chose for my first sit of the lull period. As shooting light began to fade, I heard the distinctive snap of a branch. Straining my eyes in the direction of the sound, I caught the movement of a buck slipping along the corn. I'd already passed several larger bucks, but this one held special appeal; one of his G-2 tines shot four inches back before elbowing up. He was too much to resist.

Switching on the video camera, I filmed as much of the buck's approach as I dared before shifting the camera ahead to the scent wick I'd placed when entering the stand. Bow already in hand, I drew and waited for the buck to come to a stop. The scent did its job well, stopping him cold. With his nose glued to the wick, I had plenty of time to focus on slipping the arrow neatly behind his shoulder. Several bounds and one loud crash later, the buck was mine.

Several factors played into this success. First, I prepared the stand well before the season, allowing the deer plenty of time to forget my intrusion. (When that isn't possible, it's critical to minimize the odors and disturbances created in preparing a stand.) Next, I allowed my entrance route to dictate how close to get. In that case, I felt confident I could get to within 30 yards of the field without spooking deer. As much as it would have been nice to be able to shoot into the standing corn, I didn't feel I could safely get there. Along those lines, the wind was blowing out of the bedding area, not allowing human odor to alert its occupants. Lastly, I waited until daylight movement away from bedding areas was exhausted.

Conclusion

When hunted correctly, the lull period in each season can produce nice bucks. But it's generally not a time for highly aggressive tactics. Those can come later, when the bucks are on their feet more in daylight and their minds are distracted by the rut.

RON SINFELT

A Time for Scrapes

SCRAPE HUNTING NOT PAYING OFF? TRY THIS ADVICE.

As frustrating as the lull period can be, its end brings on my favorite phase of deer season. Being in mature bucks during the two-week period before serious chasing begins is my idea of heaven on earth. At this point, the testosterone levels in their blood supply are starting to have an effect. Most likely, a doe or two has already gone through estrus. If some other buck beat the big guy to the punch, chances are high that the loser at least got a sniff, leaving him eager to breed the next doe that comes into heat.

The combination of early does and increased testosterone inspires bucks to aggressively try to establish their place in the herd hierarchy. All of this encourages them to get up a little earlier in the afternoon and stay out a little later in the morning than had been the case a mere week before. Best of all, they're still loosely clinging to predictable movement patterns. During this phase of the season, I pound scrapes hard.

When I was younger, hunting scrapes was frustrating. I'd find a large scrape, hang a stand, and have no doubt I'd be shooting a buck there the first sit. Well, the first sit would come and go, as would the second, the third and the fourth. By the time I'd finally pull my stand, the excitement I'd initially felt was replaced by utter frustration. From giving seminars to thousands of hunters over the years, I've learned that I was far from alone in this feeling of frustration.

As is the case with most other things related to hunting, the key to turning it around was analyzing what I was doing wrong. From that, I modified my approach to increase success. In short, I have found that consistent success lies in finding a scrape that is the right type and is located in an area likely to see daylight movement, not disturbing the area, and targeting it during the brief period when it's most productive. With that approach, I've dramatically increased my scrape-hunting success.

Finding The Right Scrape

Over the years, I've heard such terms as "boundary," "territorial," "breeding" and even "core area" to describe a scrape. Although I have no desire to argue if there is merit to such categorization, I've never been able to look at a scrape and tell if it was marking the buck's territory, designed for breeding, or serving as a boundary outline.

What I can tell is if it has been worked hard. From scouting the area, I can even gauge pretty accurately if one or more bucks consistently work it. Because of that, I have my own three-category classification system. When I look at a scrape, I classify it as "random," "transitional" or "primary."

As the name implies, random scrapes are haphazard in their occurrence in the landscape. A mature buck can make well in excess of 200 scrapes a year. Several studies have shown that we're lucky if the buck consistently reworks a dozen of them. The remaining 188 scrapes fall into the random category.

At the same time, we have immature bucks running around the woods. Much like a 13-year-old boy, he might know he likes girls but has no real idea what he's doing. So, he imitates the older boys. With no clue why he's doing it, he runs around making scrapes at random. In short, random scrapes make up the vast majority of scrapes found in the woods but are all but worthless to hunt. Once made, they're rarely looked at again.

Next, there are transitional scrapes. These are found between the maker's bedding and feeding areas, along the trail(s) he uses to get between them. When the maker is passing, he usually will stop to check his scrape, occasionally freshening it. However, because he's predominantly the sole user of the trail, he's also the primary user of the scrape. If the buck that made it is a shooter, these can be productive scrapes to hunt.

However, a well-placed primary scrape is my first choice every time. These scrapes are like billboards beside roadways. They're meant to relay information to as many passersby as possible. From a scrape, it's theorized that another deer can tell the sex, dominance, readiness to breed, and health of the last deer to mark it. It's much like a stop at a small-town coffee shop. Shortly after walking through the door, you know more about what the other locals have been up to than you could find out elsewhere in a year.

The author makes note of a large scrape. Even a pawing of this size might not represent a great stand site; it depends on a number of factors. Photo courtesy of Steve Bartylla.

Because their purpose is to relay information, the most heavily used primary scrapes are found near hubs of deer concentrations. Some good examples are the edges of food sources, family group bedding areas, heavily used trails, along access roads through the woods, and locations where multiple trails crisscross. Best of all, unless deer patterns change or the licking branch is destroyed, they occur in the same locations year after year after year. Why? Because these are the best places for a buck to advertise.

The next logical question is, how do we go about classifying scrapes? During hunting season, it can be tough. Often, by the time the scrape is worked to the point of our being able to classify it, the bucks have abandoned it in favor of investigating the does. On the other hand, scrapes are easily identified in the spring. And because they occur in the same locations each year, you can bet one of these scrapes will be there again the following fall.

A Time for Scrapes

When finding scrapes in the spring, key on those that have bowl-shaped appearances. The larger and/or deeper the bowl, the more attention it received. When it falls along a lone travel corridor connecting food and bedding, it's a transitional scrape. If it's at a hub of whitetail activity, chances are good it's a primary scrape. Just that easily, we can throw out all the random scrapes from the equation. It's spring scouting that enables us to do that.

Location, Location, Location

Finding primary scrapes is a good first step, but that's all it is. Even though bucks are moving more during daylight now, the vast majority of scraping is occurring after dark. That scrape along the edge of the field may cause your jaw to drop, but the odds of a monarch working it during legal shooting hours aren't great.

The next key to increasing our scrape-hunting success rate is targeting those that provide the greatest chance of daylight use. To do that, we typically have to get back into the woods to where the bucks feel safe. Some of the more common areas I've found that can produce are small openings in the woods, wooded ridges, pockets of mature trees along an otherwise brush-choked waterway, edges where the mature woods meets the swamp or another form of thick cover, and the prevailing downwind side of family group bedding areas.

When primary scrapes are found in those types of settings, all that's left is figuring out how to get in and out undetected. With any stand site that you desire to hunt more than once, this is critical. Scrape hunting is no exception. Simply put, if you can't figure out how to get back and forth without busting deer, you can't hunt it. However, with a good route, a primary scrape and a location deer feel safe in, we're beginning to see the finish line.

Getting A Jump On Scrapes

Spring isn't only good for classifying scrapes. This is a great time to prepare our stand sites. Let's face facts: It might not be impossible to slip preparing a stand site by a cagey old buck during the season, but it's far from easy. This is almost as true during the scraping phase as it was while hanging stands around a buck's bedding area during the lull period. Between the two, we have the two most challenging situations for hanging stands without being detected. When bucks are investigating scrapes, their sense of smell is on hyper-alert. Even if the changes we made to the area go unseen, a wind flowing from our new stand site to the scrape can easily give us away.

That adds up to spring being an exceptionally good time to hang stands. Also, because we'll be hunting it after the leaves drop, the cover and shooting windows will look similar to when we're hunting it. That makes it easy to gauge the level of available cover for stands, or the lack thereof, along with showing how much clearing will be necessary. Although I never clear huge shooting lanes, conducting this activity in the spring gives me the confidence to safely clear 3-foot-wide lanes in front, back and to the sides of the stand. Of course, get the landowner's permission before cutting anything, and never do so on public lands where it's not legal. In areas where theft or legal issues are a concern, you can remove the stand when you're finished.

When selecting a tree, I look for the one best suited to hide me, that just happens to sit around 20 yards on the prevailing downwind side of the scrape. This placement allows me to shoot to the scrape, as well as catch bucks that are scent-checking it from as far as 50 yards downwind of the scrape.

With all of this accomplished, we're positioned to hunt completely unsuspecting bucks. Obviously, because the clearing and tree preparation are completed, even if the stand had to be removed, all that's required is showing up, slapping in a stand, and hunting. Assuming the entrance route is good, the result is the bucks being totally ignorant to your presence. The importance of that can't be overstated.

Timing Is Everything

The stage is now set for success. All that's left is timing our hunt. After the lull and before chasing begins in earnest, there's a two-week window in which we want to be covering primary scrapes.

Scrapes can look hot well before this time frame. Actually, it's not uncommon for mature bucks to begin scraping as early as August. Uncharacteristically early scrapes are a good indication that a truly mature animal is in the area. As I write this, my brother, Joe, has a 7 1/2-year-old buck that for the last two years has started scraping up the land around his cabin in July. Middle-of-the-night Trail Master photos of this incredible monster are the only sightings thus far.

That last sentence holds the key as to why we want to wait. Every photo of the buck has come after dark. Sure, scrapes can look very impressive before this phase of the season. However, the testosterone levels in bucks haven't risen to the point where the animals are moving much during daylight. Yes, there are exceptions to everything, but the odds dictate that we wait.

I'm an odor-control fanatic. It takes me well over 30 minutes to go through my odor-reduction routine each time before I step into the woods to hunt. I meticulously try to think of every single object I bring in the woods with me and somehow treat it for odors. Every time out, I wash my glasses in hydrogen peroxide. My bow and arrows are washed once a week. A release identical to the one I practice with is used exclusively for hunting. Everything is drenched in Scent Killer, and I frequently double up on Scent-Lok garments. I wash my rubber boots, inside and out, using doe urine on boot pads or wearing Elimitrax to stop deer from busting my trail. I could do a complete book on everything I go through in

If you're going to hunt scrapes, take special care to avoid contaminating the spot with your odor. Photo courtesy of Steve Bartylla.

eliminating odors alone. Until the late season rolls around, I honestly don't hunt the wind, and to my knowledge I never get winded. However, after all of that, I'm not foolish enough to believe I can repeatedly go back and forth from most stands without the deer eventually figuring it out.

Each time we travel to the stand, we're risking educating deer to our mission of harvesting them. There are situations in which repeated trips can be pulled off, but that's a later chapter in this book. In most situations, the best we can do is minimize the risk. One important way that's accomplished is by not hunting a stand until our odds of coming out with the buck are reasonably good. Waiting until the beginning of this two-week window accomplishes that. On the flip side, changing stand strategies once the chasing begins also keeps our odds more favorable.

Once serious chasing begins, bucks aren't overly interested in tending scrapes. Certainly, they can be harvested around scrapes on either side of this brief period, but without a doubt, the most productive time is during the two-week window described here. That's when I'll be sitting by primary scrapes.

Juicing Scrape Sites

As productive as scrape hunting is during this phase, we can make it even better. Introducing mock scrapes next to primary scrapes is one way of accomplishing this. The closer we get to our window, the more we can play with a buck's brain. Two thoughts are currently dominating his mind: He wants does, and he wants to cement his place in the pecking order. With mock scrapes, we can prey on both weaknesses.

About five days before you intend on hunting a primary scrape, introduce a mock scrape, juiced with dominant buck urine. Doing so sends the message that a heavy hitter has entered the area and is intent on stealing the big guy's does.

If that isn't enough to send him over the top, spraying some estrous scent in the mock scrape gives him another nudge toward the edge. Now he not only has to contend with the new buck, but there's a" hot" doe working the stranger's scrape! This can't be tolerated.

To create this illusion, I enlist the help of the Ultimate Scrape Dripper. Hanging one above the scrape allows me to fill it with 1 1/2 ounces of Mega-Tarsal Plus. With that, the scrape will be freshened each day for a period of one to two weeks, without my having to make extra trips in to do it manually. As an added bonus, it only dispenses scent during daylight hours, offering further incentive for the buck to visit in shooting light.

When hunting scrapes by family group bedding areas, the icing on the cake is a scent trail of Special Golden Estrus, run from below my stand, through the scrape and to the bedding area. When approaching the stand, it's important to freshen the drag every 15 to 20 yards. Doing this will keep the scent getting stronger as the stand is approached. Once you hit the scrape, stop freshening the rag. That way, the scent will naturally get weaker as you approach the bedding area. The result is the trailing getting weaker the farther we get from the scrape, inspiring bucks to follow it toward our scrape. Scent trails are effective from this phase all the way to the other side of the rut.

When a good scent trail is paired with a mock scrape and a primary scrape, the setting is primed for our two-week window. That was the case when I encountered a beautiful Missouri buck. With the timing and conditions right for the hunt, I left a scent trail through the mock scrape all the way to the edge of the family group bedding area.

After I'd spent several hours seeing nothing but squirrels, a weak weather front rolled in. Unexpected fronts and switching winds are some of the reasons I take odor reduction so seriously. As the wind now blew directly into the bedding area, I banked on my efforts protecting me.

Mere moments later, I heard the first grunt coming from the bedding area. Slowly turning in that direction, I saw him. As the buck followed the scent trail with his nose to the ground, it took only one glance to see he was a shooter.

My heart sank as he stopped in the exact spot where the breeze detector indicated he'd intersect any unwanted odors. As the buck slowly raised his head, I couldn't help but question if I'd somehow

When bucks are actively scraping, they rely heavily on their noses. It's a great time to use scents on your hunts. Photo courtesy of Steve Bartylla.

allowed enough odor to slip through to ruin this otherwise perfect event. The relief I felt as he turned to watch a doe mill behind him was tremendous. After the buck horseshoed his body just enough to provide a broadside shot at his vitals, I let the arrow fly. A short 40-yard run later, the deer dropped.

Conclusion

Scrapes can be mystifying, and for many hunters they're frustratingly unproductive. Sometimes it's because the wrong location is being hunted; in other instances, the hunter simply isn't in his stand at the right time. However, when we stack everything in our favor, scrape hunting can be tremendously rewarding.

RON SINFELT

Wait Out the Chase

WHEN BUCKS WILL DO ANYTHING FOR A DOE, SIT TIGHT.

Hearing a twig snap, Trevor Wilson kicked into alert mode. It was 9 a.m., and my cameraman had yet to see his first deer of the morning. But that was about to change.

Scanning the dense tangle of brush, Trevor made out a buck trotting through the family group bedding area, searching for a doe to harass. Apparently the buck didn't like the companionship of the one he'd found. In moments, Trevor saw the doe, scurrying away from her suitor. Although the hunter had never seen the buck while hunting or on any of his trail camera's pictures, he knew immediately that this was the one he wanted.

"I had asked Steve to come out and scout our property with me that spring," Trevor responded when I asked him to summarize his hunt. "From hunting the property for several years, I felt pretty good about our stands, but it never hurts to get another perspective. During the times I spent filming his hunts, he had proven to me that he was good at quickly breaking down a property and finding the best spots. I felt pretty good when he pointed out what he believed were the best stands. Except for one, we had already selected them ourselves.

"The one we had passed on was a brush-choked tip of a ridge," Trevor continued. "Because a lot of the property's does bedded there, we were concerned that hunting it would either turn them nocturnal or cause them to relocate to a neighboring property. Steve agreed, but believed I could safely hunt it a handful of times. He went on to further convince me that, as long as I would only be taking a couple of shots, I might as well take them when the chances are the highest of connecting.

Trevor Wilson's buck was shot chasing a doe through her bedding area on the tip of a brushy ridge. Photo by Steve Bartylla.

"Having many times seen does head for thick cover when being chased, I agreed that the chase phase would be my best chance," Trevor added. "If I got into stand an hour before sunrise, worked at eliminating odors, waited for the right wind and prepared for an all-day sit, I figured it could pay off. I never dreamt it would pay off this well. I arrowed my largest buck to date on the second sit."

After Trevor watched the buck chase the doe in circles through the thick brush, several times within spitting distance of the tree stand, the buck presented a shot. Hitting his estrous-doe call, the archer was able to stop the monarch at 30 paces. With a small window leading to the deer's vitals, Trevor pulled off the perfect shot, and 80 yards later the buck crumpled.

Upon showing his trophy buck to a neighbor, Trevor learned that the deer had been living on a piece of ground nearly a mile away from the successful stand site. The buck had wandered into that bedding area with one purpose: to find an early doe to breed.

Diving Into Bedding Areas

I began this chapter with Trevor's hunt because it perfectly summarizes my philosophy on hunting the chase phase. It consists of finding the thickest bedding cover in the area and pulling all-day sits. And I firmly believe that the chase phase — the week or two before serious breeding activity occurs — is the most productive time of all to sit the entire day.

During the rut, a buck searches for a receptive doe until he finds one. When that happens, he holes up with her for around 48 hours before moving on to find the next. In areas with good nutrition, so many does come into heat at once during the peak breeding phase that finding one isn't nearly as hard for the buck as it was during the chase phase. Because there were so few does in heat early, the buck had to work much harder to find one then. In turn, that resulted in far fewer bucks spending the midday hours bedded with their prize. Combine that with the mature buck's desperation to score early, and you have the best daylight buck movement of the entire hunting season.

Furthermore, I believe the most productive locations for intercepting that buck are the thickest, nastiest bedding areas used by family groups of does and fawns. Up to this point in the season, mature bucks tend not to overly harass does that aren't ready for breeding. Although young bucks might chase does at random, the big boys tend to give them a quick sniff and then leave them alone. That changes dramatically during the chase phase. Because so many does are on the cusp of being ready, just when bucks' tremendous desire to breed and testosterone levels are peaking, even mature bucks get whipped into a frenzy. The result is a mad chasing of almost every female deer.

While this is going on with the bucks, the majority of the does still aren't quite ready. In a handful of days, many will gladly accept the advances of bucks, but not yet. In an attempt to avoid their suitors, the does typically head for the thickest bedding cover they can find and lie low. When the bucks come crashing in, the does lead them in zigzag circles, doing their best to lose them. If and when a doe is finally driven out, the bucks often make a mad dash to the next thicket and repeat the process.

On the other hand, the bucks are chasing them until they finally are thrown off the trail or come to the realization that it just isn't happening yet. When that occurs, they simply pack up shop and move to the next bedding area, hoping for better luck. The farther north we go, the more condensed and frenzied this phase becomes.

Considerations For Hunting Bedding Areas

Knowing where to be and why to be there is only the first step. As mentioned in Chapter 2, hunting close to bedding areas offers its share of challenges, and hunting *in* them is even trickier. We must keep our disturbance of the area to a minimum. Luckily, the same steps taken when hunting the edge of a buck's bedding area can be applied to hunting inside it.

Does, unlike older bucks, often wait until after first light to return to their bedding areas. You might have noticed that in Chapter 2 I never mentioned getting to my stand early. Why not? Because experience has taught me that the vast majority of bucks return to their beds well before first light during the lull period. For that reason, I hunt their late-afternoon movement toward food sources.

That isn't the case when hunting family groups' bedding areas. With does and fawns, their tendency to reach their bedding spots later in the morning affords me the opportunity to beat them in. Reaching your stand 30 minutes before shooting light is typically adequate, as it's not uncommon for family groups to arrive several hours after first light. As when hunting a buck's bedroom, selecting a route that avoids bumping deer is important. To do so, you must map a path that avoids the areas where they could be feeding.

Although beating the does in is easier, staying free of scent is more difficult. Not only do we have to remain undetected as the does pass, but we must also do so while they camp out around us. That makes taking thorough steps to eliminate odors even more critical. For those who don't, selecting a tree that's best suited for a given wind direction, along with only hunting on days when the wind is favorable and steady, is key. This often necessitates selecting a tree that isn't as strategically placed to intercept movement as it is to taking advantage of the prevailing wind direction. The saving grace to this is that the does often lead bucks throughout the thicket, potentially providing a shot opportunity anywhere within it.

Another consideration is that the hunter is frequently faced with having to sit the entire day. As stated, I believe this is the best time to do so. However, this tactic can force our hand to remain in stand, as well. When does bed around us, it becomes impossible to slip out undetected. If we leave anyway, the does will peg our stand, rendering it all but worthless. Therefore, if we want the option of hunting it again, we must prepare for a dawn-to-dusk sitting.

Going in unprepared is setting yourself up for failure. Luckily, taking a few preparatory steps can help you make it the entire day. First, as uncouth as it might seem to discuss, we must stack the odds against the need to have a bowel movement during hunting hours. I've found that eating light the day before, along with getting up extra early, works for me.

Is there any harm done by urinating from the stand? This question has been debated often. I can say that I've done it myself and have subsequently seen a mature buck sniff the spot without concern. Truth be told, I've urinated in many of my own mock scrapes. I have little doubt that, once human urine has broken down, its presence on the ground does no harm at all. However, I've also had does turn inside out upon whiffing my fresh urine. Because of that, I carry an adequately sized, sealable container.

While I've never understood why some hunters feel the need to carry food for a two- or three-hour sit, I do take some granola bars with me on all-day sits. Apple slices are another good choice. To my knowledge, neither odor has caused a deer to bolt from my stand. Finally, a container of water always accompanies me on all-day sits. Without it, the afternoon hours get awfully dry. Regardless of what you choose to bring to control your hunger or thirst, be conscious of the odors it produces, as well as the noise its container creates.

Even with those steps out of the way, sitting all day can be a test of stamina.

The author arrowed this Illinois 9-pointer in early November while hunting with www.PerformanceOutdoors.com. Placing a stand downwind of a doe bedding area in a brushy finger did the trick. Steve shot the 138-inch buck at 8 a.m. in a light rain. Photo courtesy of Steve Bartylla.

Wait Out the Chase

A comfortable stand is worth far more than its weight in venison. I also find that playing mental games helps me to pass the deerless hours. Often, I'll pick objects at random, estimate their distance and test my accuracy with the rangefinder. Each time before raising the rangefinder, I carefully survey the area for undetected deer. Another game I play is to stand for a half-hour, sit for five minutes and stand for another half-hour. As silly as this exercise sounds, it gives me something to look forward to.

Finally, though maybe I shouldn't, I've read books while on stand. In my own defense, I only do this when conditions are ideal for hearing deer approach. Even then, I scan the area after each paragraph. If you do such a thing, find a way to allow the book to air out before bringing it in the woods. I leave mine hanging from a rafter by a string on our roofed porch for a week. When I get to my hunting location, I tie the string to my stand. That allows me to ease the book down to the side of my stand at the first sign of approaching deer.

Conclusion

Regardless of how you convince yourself to stand in your stand all day, doing so will be well worth the effort during the chase phase. More so than at any other time of hunting season, a big buck can wander by at any time. When done properly, hunting thick family group bedding areas can make this a magical time to be in the woods.

Peak Rut Strategy

RON SINFELT

Peak Rut Strategy

FIND THE DOES AND YOU'LL FIND THE BUCKS, TOO.

The rut! Few words inspire more excitement in a deer hunter. They bring visions of trophy bucks going nuts, moving at all times of the day, showing up anywhere, falling for nearly every trick in the hunter's book. Any doe that's ready is leading at least one buck around by his nose. Those bucks that aren't accompanying does are frantically searching for the next willing mate. The resulting chaos in the woods is matched only by the excitement of those who chase whitetails.

It's often said that buck movement is totally random during the most active time of the rut, and it can appear that luck, more than anything else, determines who shoots a big deer and who doesn't. But the movement isn't random, and that means there are strategies we can employ to lessen our dependence on luck.

Granted, a first impression might be that bucks suddenly exhibit no rhyme or reason to their meanderings. However, a closer look reveals that they employ a system for scent-checking the maximum number of does for a given amount of time and effort. The two most pronounced examples can be seen in how they cruise family group bedding areas and food sources in search of the right female.

Hunting Does to Hunt Bucks

Since we left the last chapter discussing hunting family group bedding areas, we might as well begin there. As opposed to the fashion in which many mature bucks plunge headfirst into these sanctuaries during the chase phase, most now skirt the downwind edges. For all that's written about rut-crazed bucks, I believe they now employ a more sensible, safety-oriented approach than is the case during the chase phase. The way I see it, the chase phase's relative lack of "hot" does, combined with an instinctive knowledge of the approaching feast, creates an almost uncontrollable frenzy in a buck's brain. However, much like the seasoned veteran pitcher during the World Series, the mature buck knows when it's crunch time.

During the rut, an older buck understands that skirting the downwind side of a family group bedding area allows him to scent-check every occupant in almost

In the author's view, the best rut funnels lie between two or more areas heavily used by does. Photo by Ron Sinfelt.

no time, allowing him to continue on if none is ready to breed. Therefore, it only stands to reason that bedding areas inhabited by family groups of does and fawns are good locations in which to ambush mature rutting bucks.

When selecting these stand sites for the rut, I focus on covering the most heavily used trails on the downwind side of the family group bedding area. To narrow it down even farther, the best placement is typically about 20 yards from the edge. Doing this allows for catching bucks scent-checking from as much as 50 yards downwind of the does (farther with a firearm), along with the possibility of a buck using the covered trail alone or having a doe lead him down it.

A faint trail downwind of a doe bedding area can yield a buck in rut. Photo by Gordon Whittington.

These setups are also ideally suited for using estrous scents. With the buck desperately wanting to find a receptive doe, a scent wick or trail of estrous urine leading past the stand is often enough to dupe him. Simply put, he already has his mind fixed on finding a "hot" doe, desperately wanting to believe one is there for him. As a result, he's much more easily duped. By using estrous scents, along with harnessing this placement strategy, the hunter is stacking the odds in his favor.

This same systematic approach to finding receptive does applies to cruising food sources. By doing nothing more than circling the food source, a buck can scent-check every doe that has visited as much as 48 hours prior. When the buck stumbles across the track of a doe that's ready, all he must do is follow her scent. This is perhaps the most effective way for a buck to check the largest number of does in the least amount of time.

Keep in mind that, although rutting bucks sometimes seem to have lost all regard for personal safety, that isn't entirely true. To help conceal themselves, they rarely make this loop through an open crop field. Instead, they most often skirt it five to 40 yards inside the woods. Staying close retains the concentration of doe activity that the source provides and allows them to visually check for both does and danger while remaining hidden.

To fully capitalize on this, stands should be placed 15 to 20 yards inside the woods. Not only does this provide shot opportunities at bucks that are skirting the food source, it also affords a view of the field. As much as most bucks cherish safety, weird things do happen during the rut. If a monarch saunters across the middle of the field, this stand placement will allow the hunter to see him. If the hunter is using a firearm, the deer might already be within range; if the hunter is using a bow, he might be able to give a sexy enough doe call to lure the buck close.

Taking stand placement a bit further, it's a good idea to also cover a heavily used family group trail. As with the bedding-area setup, this allows for intercepting bucks that are using the trail alone, as well as those that might be following a doe to the food. Luckily for us, the best trails often are on inside corners of a field, providing the further benefit of funneling traveling bucks that aren't checking the field. Bucks wanting to get from one side of the field to the other without going through the open food source will cut the corners. When all of these factors are combined, this setup takes a lot of the blind luck out of harvesting a rutting buck.

Plugging The Funnel

Our last placement strategy also takes advantage of the rutting buck's doe-seeking ways. Assuming they aren't already with does, it's no great secret that the majority of bucks greatly expand their home range and travel more in daylight during the rut. As much as they focus their efforts on locating receptive does, putting on miles is usually still a prerequisite. Their travels take them from one doe group to the next, pushing on until they run out of gas or find what they seek.

Obviously, hunting funnels can be highly productive during this phase of the season. By nature, funnels are nothing more than habitat, manmade or topographical features that focus deer activity through a relatively narrow passageway. A finger of woods that connects two woodlots, a brush-choked stream meandering through an open pasture, a brushy fencerow separating two fields, and an inside corner of a field are all examples of habitat funnels. A manmade funnel might be where a road pinches the woods closer to a lake, a low spot in an otherwise well-maintained fence, or a mature slice of woods left between two new clearcuts.

Some common examples of topographical funnels are a low spot in a ridge (saddle), a flat section that runs along the mid-point of a steep sidehill or ridge (bench), the upper and lower ends of steep cuts that slice up the side of a ridge, a strip of dry land separating two wetlands, or a relatively flat spot in an otherwise steep river bank. The lay of the land makes each of these funnels the path of least resistance for traveling deer.

In most cases, these funnels can be avoided if a deer wishes to do so. However, the cost is that the deer must expend more energy and/or expose itself to greater danger to avoid the area. Because bucks have no desire to waste energy or expose themselves to unneeded dangers, the funnels are their best option.

Superior rut funnels are those that separate areas used by two or more clans of does and fawns. A great example of this setup is a stand I hung several years back. A deep cut sliced uphill through the woods, stopping only 50 yards short of the field atop the ridge. On one side of the cut was a large block of timber; on the other was a 200-yard-wide swath of wooded sidehill containing numerous family group bedding areas. With the cut running all the way down to the field below, the deer had three options: (1) expend extra energy crossing the deep cut; (2) circle through the open field above or below the cut; or (3) loop around just above the cut's upper end, staying hidden in the woods as they did.

My last sit on the tip was on one of those mornings deer hunters live for. I had no more than settled into my stand when I heard the stiff-legged walk of a buck approaching. I made out the silhouette of a young buck grunting his way toward me, and moments after passing, he began chasing every doe he found. That was merely the beginning of the nearly nonstop action to come.

Several hours later, I again heard the sound of a trotting deer approaching my stand. The nicest buck of the morning was coming my way, and fast. His body told me he was mature, but his short, dagger-like tines fooled me. I had just decided to pass on him when he turned his head. In that one moment, I realized the mistake I'd been about to make. The decent mass of the main beams and his 22-inch inside spread won the debate in an instant.

Having very little time to react, I twisted and grabbed my bow from its holder. Luckily for me, the buck didn't catch the speed at which I swung my body back and then came to full draw. When the buck hit a scent wick doused in Special Golden Estrus, he stopped, and I released the arrow. In fewer than 10 sits, that stand has produced close encounters with seven trophy-class whitetails for me.

Rut Stand Considerations

Before closing out this chapter, let's cover some random points that can help us make the most of the rut. To begin with, during the rut scents serve an even more important role than drawing bucks into shooting range. As was the case with the buck in the hunt just described, the right scents have the ability to stop that trotting buck in his tracks, providing time for a relaxed and ethical shot.

Most lone bucks are on a mission during the rut. One second, the woods are dead . . . the next, a buck is trotting by. Grunting can bring the buck to a stop, but having seen several turn inside out at a grunt issued too close for comfort, I've come to prefer stopping them with scent. I now place scent wicks of estrous urine in my shooting lanes. This is enough to stop bucks in most cases, by providing them something to focus on other than me. The right scent also has the power to both draw them in and position them for the shot. Because of all of those key factors working together, I rarely hunt the rut without using estrous scent.

Along those lines, right before, during and immediately after the breeding phases of the season are when calling, rattling, decoying and using scents are all most effective. When used properly, each plays to what the buck's mind is already set on. Because this book is dedicated to stand-hunting, I won't go into great detail on these topics. However, it's important to point out that using all four together goes a long way toward fooling the buck's eyes, nose and ears. When this is combined with the timing of the buck's mind already hoping to find the lie you're selling him, it can be tremendous in strengthening your odds of success.

While I believe the chase phase is most productive for all-day sits, don't discount hunting from daylight until dark during the breeding phase. Many mature bucks might already be paired up with does, but the ones that aren't typically put on miles each day. That translates into a day of potentially going from boredom to excitement in seconds. Also, because they're traveling farther now than at any other time, if that Booner comes through while you're sitting at the restaurant eating lunch, chances are you'll never see him again. He could easily be a mile or two away before you climb back into the stand for your afternoon hunt.

Conversely, there's also an advantage to having bucks move through. Although you might only have one chance at any specific buck, one that was three miles away yesterday could come trotting by at any second. This constant exchange of mature bucks inspires me to hunt my best stands hard during the rut. You never want to educate deer, but the buck that busts your track today will most likely be long gone tomorrow anyway . . . with a different one appearing to take his place. This is the one and only time of the season when I'm not tempted to give up a stand location because a buck has busted me in it. As long as I can keep the does ignorant of my intrusion, I'll hunt my best stands every day of the rut.

Conclusion

Hunting the rut can be like plunging yourself into chaos. Yet, if we remember what the bucks are after, we can put ourselves in position to intercept a great many more of them. By hunting family group bedding areas, food sources and funnels, we're taking advantage of a buck's own methods of finding does. Once we stack the odds further in our favor through all-day sits, using aggressive tactics and relying on scents to increase our shot opportunities, we've effectively removed much of the "luck" factor from filling our tag with a rutting monarch.

The Second Rut

RON SINFELT

The Second Rut

RUN-DOWN BUCKS STILL HAVE LOVE ON THEIR MINDS.

I once felt tremendous envy when reading stories about the second rut. Growing up in northern Wisconsin, I believed this was a magical time enjoyed only by deer hunters in states south of my own.

I had reason to feel this way. As opposed to the southernmost states and Mexico, where some form of rutting activity can be seen for months after the primary rut, breeding time is much more condensed in the North. Here, the critical timing of spring birth demands that the vast majority of does be impregnated in a fairly narrow window of time. If a doe is bred too early, her fawns might be born during the tail end of harsh weather conditions. Any fawn born while snow still covers the ground or when the temperature is below 10 degrees Fahrenheit would face drastically reduced odds of survival.

The same is true if the fawn is born late. In that case, it doesn't have the time to grow as much before the hormones kick in to halt growth and inspire fat production. If the snow depths are significant that winter, not only is being small a handicap for travel, but it also reduces the fawn's ability to reach as high to eat the buds on trees. The result is an animal that must expend more energy to travel, yet isn't able to compete as well for nutrition. Obviously, that's a bad combination when straddling the line between life and death.

Now, all of this must be combined with the fact that Northern deer can't intake the same potential amount of nutrition over the course of a year that deer living in areas lacking long-term snow cover can. For example, even in Illinois a fawn has a fighting chance of being able to feed on greens, acorns and the waste in farm fields until some point in January. By contrast, in much of the species' Northern range, not only are there vast areas void of farming, but

In a well-nourished herd, a significant percentage of doe fawns will come into heat. This typically occurs a month or more after the primary rut, resulting in a sudden burst of concentrated buck activity. Photo by Ron Sinfelt.

the much earlier average snowfall often buries any remaining morsels of food at ground level, leaving less-nutritious woody browse as the fawns' best choice.

With the healthiest fawns making up most of the second rut in the Upper Midwest and points northward, the increased nutrition that occurs as we travel to the mid-regions of the U.S. allows a higher percentage of female fawns to come into estrus. Of course, in the areas where droughts and poor soil hamper the available level of nutrition, a reduction in the percentage of fawns that come into estrus occurs as well.

Amazingly, despite the hurdles facing Northern deer, some fawns typically do come into estrus each year. Even in the Upper Peninsula of Michigan, where excessive snowfall and frigid temperatures are the norm, an average of 5 percent of doe fawns come into estrus early in their first winter. The point is that despite my youthful belief that the second rut didn't exist in the Northern regions, it does. It's just far less noticeable than in areas experiencing milder winters.

Another factor that helps mask the North's second rut is the drastic reduction in rutting-buck activity. Much like fawns that try to survive their first winter, the bucks are also handicapped. Having burned 25 to 30 percent of their body weight during the rigors of the rut, mature bucks must now contend with trying to survive winter. Because their fat reserves are depleted, they simply can no longer afford to invest their energies covering miles and miles of ground each day. If they did, chances are that it would cost them their lives.

Instead, they're primarily focused on conserving energy. Commonly, this involves setting up reduced home ranges hinging upon the best remaining food sources. Luckily for the bucks, the family groups are now concentrated around them as well. Because of that, bucks can spend most of the day resting and still check a good number of fawns at the food source in late afternoon. When one of the local girls enters womanhood, you can bet that the area's bucks will be competing to win her favors.

Of course, with the rarity of a week of freezing temperatures and snow cover in the South, deer residing there don't face the same obstacles. In the South, adult does have the luxury of being able to rear fawns born very early or even late. (Summer drought that limits a doe's milk production is the chief threat to many Southern fawns.) Because of that wide range in birth dates, along with a host of other contributing factors, does are bred for a much longer window of time, blurring the lines between a first and second rut essentially into one elongated rut.

Hunting Strategies

In the Deep South, stand-placement strategies really don't change much after the first does come into estrus. Although the comparative lack of breeding intensity might result in funnels receiving less buck travel for a typical day of the rut, funnels are often still good choices on the last day of season. The same holds true for catching bucks prowling family group bedding areas and scent-checking food sources. All three locations are still good choices for stand sites.

However, that's not the case in the Upper Midwest or elsewhere in the North. In fact, for those of you who hunt areas in which deer commonly yard up during the winter, the best options for tagging a buck after the first rut will be found in the next chapter. Frankly, even those who hunt the more southern parts of the North and Upper Midwest would be best served to spend the remaining days of the season alternating between the tactics about to be described here and those in the following chapter.

As you'll find is the case during the post-rut, the best bet of tagging bucks during the second rut lies in shifting our stands to the hottest food source the area holds and then keying on the areas within the food source that are seeing the most concentrated feeding activity. Certainly there are times when the bruiser will still check the family group's bedding area, but unless continued hunting pressure has soured him on daylight visits to the food source, cruising bedding areas no longer wins the risk/reward comparison. In most settings, the odds of catching him at the food source are better and offer less risk of altering the deer's patterns.

That's not to say hunting food sources is without risk. Even more so than earlier in the season, routes to and from the stand, being properly concealed and not getting winded are challenges. To make it worse, frozen ground and reduced living plant material both reduce natural odors that help mask our own. Throw in the fact that the surviving deer have already made it through the brunt of the "war," and our prey is now far less tolerant of our intrusions.

Sure, in areas of limited forage options, it might take a lot to drive deer completely away from using a prime food source. However, the slightest trace of danger sends them dashing for cover faster than at any time earlier in the season. Where before the old doe might have eventually disregarded a flicker of movement or a slight trace of odor after a brief investigation, now she will stare, test the wind, stomp, stare and repeat the process until, more often than not, she blows and flees for cover, only to spend the next 10 minutes snorting in the woods. It doesn't take many of these world-alerting encounters to convince the local deer that coming out after dark is a better idea.

All of this makes selecting stand sites that provide good access routes, cover and placement for the wind of critical importance. After the first rut, far more than during any other phase of the season, I'll sacrifice a stand that offers superior placement for intercepting deer for one that provides better odds of going undetected. Far too many late afternoons filled with snorting deer have taught me that lesson well.

The saving grace to selecting stands that are slightly off from where we really would like to be is that deer seldom enter a food source and camp in one location.

They tend to spread out, milling around as they feed. At the same time, the more mature bucks often feel compelled to visit each new doe that enters the food source. In doing so, the bucks often cover much of the area, presenting shot opportunities that otherwise wouldn't be there.

Luckily, there are tactics that we can use to draw bucks to our stand. The combination of still being interested in breeding and far fewer receptive females being available makes bucks susceptible to estrous scents. Placing several doc-

Whether a second-rut buck is still looking for a girlfriend or just wants to fill his belly, he'll head for the best remaining food source in the area. In the weeks immediately after the primary rut, a stand near the edge of a field or other feeding area can be a winner. Photo by Ron Sinfelt.

tored scent wicks around our stand, as well as laying a scent trail leading to it, can bring into shooting range bucks that otherwise might have continued to feed too far away.

Using decoys is yet another way of drawing in bucks. However, if they're surrounded by does, traditional decoys can do more harm than good. Given that does already have a hair trigger at this time, an up-close look at a motionless decoy often sends them running.

Using the decoy as a buck can help to avoid this. Because most does don't want to be harassed, they commonly steer clear of bucks. On the other hand, the mature bucks typically like to introduce themselves to the new guy. It's the big buck's own special way of letting the intruder know that he's the man and that the new guy had best mind his manners. When paired with the use of both dominant buck and estrous urines, a buck decoy can bring results. However, because of bucks' still-burning urge to breed, a doe decoy and estrous urine combination works best. One way to avoid getting it busted by does is to set it in a less-used portion of the feeding area. Hopefully, a buck's urge to check every doe will pull him away from the other deer and into shooting range.

A better alternative is using the RoboCoy. Produced by Custom Robotic Wildlife in Mosinee, Wisconsin, it's essentially a full-body mount of a deer. Made with real deer hide covering a foam frame, it has built-in robotics that allow for remote-controlled movement of the head and tail. It's the only decoy I've ever used that can consistently withstand close inspections from family groups and put them at ease, along with being a deadly draw for bucks.

(Obviously, hunter safety is of paramount concern whenever using decoys, particularly those that are extremely lifelike. Standard advice is to restrict their use to archery-only seasons and private property where the user can be confident no other hunter will mistake the decoy for a real deer.)

Conclusion

By using scents and decoys and/or relying on proper stand placement around the best available feeding areas, we can score during the second rut. The added advantage of this placement strategy is that it also lets us get close to bucks that don't have any remaining visible interest in does. Because the bucks still must recuperate from the rigors of the rut, they rely heavily on prime food sources. Hunting stand sites bordering food gives us a chance to capitalize on either of those possibilities.

RON SINFELT

Post-Rut Success

IT TAKES PLENTY OF CLOTHES AND A WINNING PLAN.

Snatching my bag of clothes and gear from the truck, I headed into the woods. Upon reaching a safe location, I began the unpleasant task of changing. Racing to slip on a layer of thermals, I longed for the days when the temperature had been above single digits.

After stashing my driving clothes, I slipped on my Scent-Lok liner, topped it with camo, doused myself with Scent Killer, and was ready to rock. Following a short walk and 20-foot climb up the tree, I was just settling in when the first group of does and fawns came pouring into the picked cornfield.

It was late December, a full three hours before dark, and I already had seven deer within 50 yards. As the first two hours zipped by, more deer piled down the ridge on the opposite side of the narrow cornfield. Soon, the field was crawling with deer pawing for the snow-covered kernels. My attention was focused on a group of three yearlings and a 2 1/2-year-old 8-pointer I had seen the five previous days.

Suddenly, a little 6-pointer's head shot up to look at the ridge. As the yearling assumed a submissive posture, I knew the big boy was about to appear.

A mere glance from the large-bodied 9-pointer sent the small buck scurrying away. Confidently swaggering to the middle of the field, still a good 60 yards from me, the big buck began filling his belly. Gripping my bow tightly, I argued with myself. Should I try to grunt him over, or wait him out? The last two afternoons, I'd chosen the safe route. With so many sets of eyes on the field, I was concerned that drawing any attention to myself would be too much of a risk. Finally, I decided that if he didn't make it over by the time gray light came, I'd use the low light to help conceal me when I called.

About 10 minutes later, I caught the break I needed. The 8-pointer began harassing a little forkhorn. After playfully sparring, he got too aggressive for the little guy and chased him near my stand. Securing the release to my bowstring loop, I positioned my feet for what I hoped would happen next.

The big guy, with his attention focused on the pair from the start, puffed up and began stomping his way over. Hoping the scrappy 8-pointer would stand fast, I raised my bow and readied for the shot. At 20 yards the 9-pointer altered his head-on approach to make eye contact with his subordinate. Coming to full draw, I settled the pin behind the big deer's shoulder and released.

In an instant, the buck exploded into the air, kicking violently before bursting across the field. Slanting farther to the side with each yard he covered, he horseshoed his body as he crumpled to the ground. On my sixth consecutive afternoon of hunting this spot, the buck was mine.

Enduring The Worst

If there's a well-kept secret in hunting mature bucks, it's how productive late season can be in regions where that time of year brings harsh weather conditions. Fortunately for those of us who enjoy late-season hunting, comparatively few other hunters take advantage of this opportunity. Perhaps it's because the other hunters have already filled their buck tags. Maybe it's that they believe every animal sporting good antlers has already been harvested. It might even relate to what an Illinois hunter once told me on a January trip: "You guys aren't really going out to hunt in this?! The highs are only in the single digits, and there's more than two feet of snow on the ground!"

If you're physically and mentally prepared for it, the post-rut can offer red-hot hunting. Photo by Gordon Whittington.

To keep him from calling the psych ward, I didn't bother to mention that the week before had seen me out in 15-below-zero temps, overlooking a cornfield covered in over three feet of snow. Funny, that Illinois trip was one of my best ever.

Truth be told, I suspect that it's a combination of all three of those factors that keeps many hunters out of the woods in late season. Another factor is that many of the stand sites that were hot before are now colder than the frigid temperatures. Speaking from experiences of my youth, I can tell you that it just isn't much fun getting frostbite while watching a patch of snow that doesn't even hold a single track. I can see how one or two of those experiences could convince a hunter to stay indoors. Hunting the post-rut offers serious challenges to overcome.

Still, compared to what the bucks themselves can be forced to endure, we hunters have it easy. The toll paid from rutting can be seen in weight loss and injury, and it couldn't occur at a worse time. Now the bucks must try to survive winter. The unlucky ones that must make it on a diet consisting mainly of woody browse do it while running a negative energy balance. Simply put, they expend more calories each day than they take in.

With the buck's fat reserves already depleted, and harsh conditions a real possibility, survival is no easy feat. Traveling through deep snows and cold temps drains a lot of energy. Even in agricultural-rich areas, snow depths of much more than a foot force deer to shift their diet to comparatively poor sources of energy. In addition, many of these deer also must contend with predators, such as timber wolves, dogs and the larger members of the cat family.

In an effort to minimize the effects of all of these detrimental factors, deer of the Upper Midwest, mountains and points farther north employ behavioral and physiological adaptations. To begin with, they significantly reduce their movement. Often, they do little more than travel back and forth between bedding and feeding locations. The less they move, the less energy they burn. To take energy conservation a step further yet, they even slow their metabolism.

Along with that, when the temperatures really plummet, the deer combat this by shifting their feeding activities more to the warmer late-afternoon hours. Since the late-night and early-morning hours are typically the coldest portion of the day, this modification allows them to remain bedded, conserving body heat, during these frigid periods.

In places where bad winter weather doesn't force deer to feed heavily in daylight, bucks and does of all ages become more nocturnal during the post-rut period. Photo by Ron Sinfelt.

Next, they shift their now greatly reduced home range to locations that best promote their survival. In the areas that consistently receive deep snow cover and brutal temperatures, the destinations for these winter migrations are traditional yarding areas. Most often, a thick stand of mature evergreens, such as white cedar or spruce, is selected. Here, the dense canopy of branches creates a ceiling effect. Not only does this trap heat to keep the temperature at ground level a degree or two warmer, it also captures some of the snow, making travel easier. Furthermore, with so many deer packing into these areas, the extra hoof traffic also results in more easily traveled deer trails, in addition to providing more noses, eyes and ears to detect predators.

In conjunction with that, this is the period when those otherwise solitary bucks now gladly utilize the same bedding areas, trails and food sources as the family groups. This intermingling allows them to take advantage of the heat-retention properties of the yarding area and increased protection from predators, as well as the easier travel that the packed trail system provides.

In this setting, the food sources are most often woody browse. White cedar is always preferred, when available. It's the only woody browse known to be able to sustain a whitetail's life completely by itself. Areas of recent logging activity are typically the next best alternative. If the logging is conducted in early winter, the plethora of tops scattered across the ground provides a bounty of buds. Older activities can be good choices, as well. Until the regrowth of saplings extend beyond the deer's reach, they also offer a concentration of tender buds. If none of those choices is available, it becomes a matter of finding whatever natural browse is available.

As we drift into areas that typically provide warmer temps and less snow cover, a less traditional form of yarding occurs. Instead of concentrating on thermal cover, deer in these regions gravitate to the best available food sources. When they exist, standing crops, such as corn, soybeans and sorghum, are almost always preferred. In areas where standing crops are in short supply, it's not uncommon for a lone field to draw deer from miles around. When snow depths allow, waste left from harvesting crops is also a good option. The same can hold true of hayfields that contain round bales of hay. When agricultural options aren't available, the same hierarchy of woody browse species polishes off the list of preferred food sources.

Interestingly, in areas where yarding commonly occurs, mild winters often inspire deer to dismiss traditional yarding areas for prime food sources, as well. However, regardless of how much better the food may be, they'll almost always choose the thermal protection when snowflakes and temperatures fall.

Not any one of these behavioral and physiological adaptations may appear to make a significant difference. But with the line between life and death being so fine, any advantage a deer can gain is important. When all of these factors are combined, they're substantial enough to significantly increase winter survival rates.

Capitalizing On Adaptations

Now that we understand how whitetails cope with winter stress, we can explore how to most efficiently use these traits to our advantage. At first glance, it may appear that drastically reduced movement is a disadvantage. However, finding where a mature buck resides swiftly transforms this into a significant advantage. Investing several late afternoons observing the listed food sources is a good way to find him. Because there's no other time during the season that a mature buck more rigidly clings to a pattern, this is well worth the effort.

With that accomplished, the next step is to backtrack his trail just far enough into the woods to allow the hunter a route to and from the stand. On the rare occasion when a safe route exists to a field-edge stand, such as in the hunt that began this chapter, this is also acceptable. In fact, it's preferred, owing to the increased odds of catching the minimal second-rut activity that might occur. This also provides a firearms hunter with the chance of a longer shot. Moreover, because the concentration effect often means that more than one mature buck is utilizing the same food source, sitting the edge often provides opportunities that in-woods trails don't. Still, without a good route, more harm than good is the most common result.

The deer's tendency to shift feeding times up is also an advantage. Frankly, deep snows and cold temps are the late-season's hunter's best friends. The worse it gets, the more inspiration the bruiser has to hit the food source before dark. This is so pronounced that these conditions can make an otherwise nearly exclusively nocturnal buck feed during daylight in an open field. Many of my best hunts have occurred on the coldest day of the season. On the flip side, unseasonably mild conditions tend to shut down a mature buck's daylight movement. If a high-risk stand site is the only option, saving it for an afternoon of brutally low temperatures is the best option.

Dealing With Adversity

Picking a good stand location is only half the battle. Next, we must conquer the elements. Luckily, advances in hunting clothing have made persevering in almost any condition possible. From countless battles with the cold, I have found two options that work. The first is investing in numerous layers of quality cold-weather clothing. Hand muffs, chemical heating packs, boot blankets and Polar Heat Exchanger Masks are all nice complements to this approach.

The other option is the Heater Body Suit. It's been my choice since the first time I used it. This cold-weather-hunting outfit not only makes those 30-degree mornings more enjoyable, but it allows the hunter to remain comfortable in temps well below zero. The advantages of staying in the stand are obvious. In short, you can't harvest a deer when you're sitting at home on the couch. Every bit as important is the fact that being comfortable keeps you focused. When your mind is dwelling on how miserable you feel, you are fidgeting more, your senses aren't keyed on hunting, and the odds of harvesting a deer plummet. The Heater Body Suit effectively removes these obstacles from late-season hunting.

With that done, you can focus on odor elimination and sound reduction for both yourself and your equipment. Thankfully, a combination of Scent-Lok and Scent Killer products can handle the odor factor, and inspecting equipment enables the hunter to address unwanted noises. Although difficult, it's hardly impossible to ambush a mature whitetail when these factors are treated with the appropriate attention. In fact, it's one of my favorite times to be in a stand.

RON SINFELT

Timing Your Hunts

**THE *WHEN* CAN BE
JUST AS CRITICAL
AS THE *WHERE*.**

With a season-long game plan for stand placement now established, it's time to shift our attention to some other fine points of stand-hunting. One is learning to time our efforts for the best odds of success.

Just as each phase of deer season has stand-placement strategies that work best, certain stands are most productive at certain times of the day. Of course, just as an early-season stand sometimes will produce in late season, a stand best suited for a morning hunt can pay off in the afternoon. The circumstances surrounding each situation must be evaluated. In deer hunting, every rule has its exceptions. We must rely on tendencies, probabilities and playing the odds.

It might surprise some readers to know that several years back, I began to question the merits of morning hunting. This was the case despite the fact that I'd been known to say, "The best time to hunt is anytime you legally can" and "You'll never shoot a buck while sitting on the couch." That's one of the things I enjoy most about hunting: One never stops learning. The day you believe you have uncovered all there is to learn, you either have something happen that humbles you into realizing you don't or your skills begin to decline.

My work with outfitters first led me to question morning hunts. It began when I started to study logs kept by Tom Indrebo of Bluff Country Outfitters in Buffalo County, Wisconsin. Tom's detailed logs of each client's daily deer sightings show that, when compared to afternoons, morning and midday sightings/harvests of mature bucks are drastically lower during the early, lull and

Jim Kostroski's Minnesota non-typical — a 214-inch giant that broke the archery world record for velvet whitetails — was shot from a tree stand on the afternoon of Sept. 13, 2003. Until the peak scraping phase, afternoons tend to be more productive than mornings. Photo by Pat Reeve.

second-rut/post-rut phases of hunting season. By "drastically," I mean somewhere around 20:1. The same trend holds true in the logs of two of my other outfitter friends: Bucks & Beards Outfitters, stationed outside of Grant City, Missouri,
and www.PerformanceOutdoors.com, which has land in Illinois and Iowa.

With few stands being positioned perfectly enough to keep from educating
deer to our hunting activity, I believe that morning hunting during these phases
tends to do more harm than good. Tom agrees wholeheartedly. "I wish my hunters
would sleep in on those days," he says. "Because they have paid for the right to
hunt, I can't discourage them from going out. I sure never discourage the ones
who want to sleep in, though.

"One of the biggest problems with morning hunting during those stages is
that the mature bucks usually bed before first light, but a lot of the times the does
and younger bucks don't," Tom explains. "That puts the hunters at risk of running into the mature bucks as they walk in during the dark, depositing odors that
any deer could find, and having to let the does and young bucks pass through
without noticing the hunter in the tree. That's a lot to risk when the chance of
shooting a mature buck is so low."

As stated, there are exceptions to this rule. Except for during the chasing
and breeding phases, getting a shot at a mature buck in the morning typically
requires hunting a stand set near his bedding area. Second, all of the conditions
must be perfect for the hunter to remain undetected, including on the way to and
from the stand. Lastly, throw in a light drizzle and the odds are better for buck
movement later in the morning. The passage of a front producing prolonged nasty
weather also can inspire a mature buck to move. When heavy rains and/or high
winds have shut down movement for a day or more, sitting in a stand that guards
the trail from his bedding spot to a secluded feeding area can produce.

It's also true that anytime heavy hunting pressure results in kicking deer
around the woods is a good time to be on stand. Under those conditions, morning stands that cover the entrance routes to protective cover are great choices.
Because other hunters are inadvertently driving deer to your location, these stand
sites can produce all day long.

Sudden Changes

As slow as those early-season mornings are for movement of mature bucks,
things change drastically as soon as the peak scraping phase begins.

"It's like someone hits a switch," Tom says. "One morning my hunters are
telling me again about all the does and little bucks they saw, and the next morning half of them are shaking from the close encounters they had with huge bucks.
When that happens, I know that the morning hunts are going to be as good as
the afternoon sits until the rut is done." Talk to Donnie McClellan of Bucks &
Beards, as well as Jake or Justin Roach at www.PerformanceOutdoors.com, and

you'll learn that their experiences concur with Tom's.

Now that the testosterone levels are inspiring the big boys to move after daylight, where are the best locations for intercepting them? First, let's look at locations that *aren't* going to be good. Regardless of the phase of the season, field-edge stands are rarely good morning choices. For one, it can be extremely challenging to get to them undetected. Next, once daylight hits, the majority of the big boys' feeding is done. Sure, they might still hit secluded and in-woods food sources, but odds are they won't feed in the middle of the alfalfa field during the day.

However, when fields separate family groups and pronounced crossing exists, these can be good locations for intercepting roaming bucks. Also, the intense pressure of firearms season can make these good spots in which to nail fleeing bucks at any time of day. This is particularly true when one side of the field possesses superior protective cover and deer caught on the other side have no other choice but to cross the opening to get to it.

During the peak scraping, chase and breeding phases of the rut, the stands outlined in those respective chapters are equally good at any time of day. Because of that, all are candidates for productive all-day sits. This is even true of rut stands that flank food sources. Because these stands are set back from the edge, a hunter's pre-dawn travel through the woods often will let him avoid any deer still feeding in the field. Furthermore, this setup is geared far more toward intercepting bucks that are scent-checking recent diners, in addition to giving the hunter a chance at bucks that are cutting inside corners as they transition between family groups. Any of those activities can result in sightings from dawn to dusk.

As mentioned, when hunting pressure is high, another prime location for all-day sits is covering the entrances to protective cover, or even right in the middle of that cover. When hunting these settings, I do all I can to use other hunters to my advantage. That means getting into place before them in the morning and staying put until the bitter end.

This approach can result in multiple peak-movement periods during the day. First, as the other firearms hunters trickle into the woods, they bounce deer like pinballs. This occurs again as hunters leave their stands for lunch or decide to go for walks. Of course, when they return for the afternoon hunt, they stir the deer all over again. In the meantime, groups of hunters might really shake things up as they conduct organized drives. Any of this can make the big boys head for the safety of the protective cover, where you just happen to be waiting for them.

Investing Midday Hours

As unproductive as mornings can be during the early, lull and second-rut/post-rut phases, midday and late-afternoon sits can be just the opposite. Many hunters sit for the first and last three hours of the day. However, the often-overlooked window between those two periods can be very productive. Having already covered the all-day sits, let's focus on how this can be applied to the early, lull and second-rut/post-rut phases.

Although I believe morning hunts typically aren't worth the risk, the midday tactic we're about to explore offers significantly reduced risk and greater odds of success.

Studies have shown that outside of the rut, five peak-movement periods occur during 24-hour periods. They occur in the early evening, twice during the night, once in the morning and around midday. Evening and morning movement periods can sway to either side of darkness as deer travel between food and bedding. The nighttime movements consist of alternating between feeding and bedding to regurgitate cud. It can also involve shifting to different food sources.

In this discussion, we're most interested in midday movement. Because of its time slot, it can't be hidden under the cover of darkness. This movement most often consists of shifting from one bedding site to either another closer to the evening's food source or a hidden feeding and bedding area. An example of the latter would be an oak ridge where acorns are dropping. A buck bedded in the thicket below could get up during the midday hours, relieve himself and then climb the ridge to feed on acorns. After having his fill, he could retire to a nearby point overlooking the valley below.

Other somewhat common hidden food sources are well-placed pockets of honeysuckle, berry brambles, isolated apple trees and sources of browse. Most often, these are supplemental food sources. Sometimes, however, they can be primary food sources,

During early season, midday hunting can be effective in secluded feeding areas. Find an acorn-laden oak near a mature buck's bedding spot and you could be in business. Photo by Ron Sinfelt.

as with acorns. Either way, they almost always offer deer a feeling of safety, owing to the protective cover or isolation they provide.

Understanding this, we can begin putting the pieces in place to find good midday stand sites. Doing this requires a thorough knowledge of a particular buck's habits. Sure, we might get lucky by blundering out and setting up on a random in-woods food source and have him show up around 11 a.m., but that's asking a lot. At the very least, knowing the buck's bedding areas allows us to deductively reason where he might head during midday.

Because in-woods food sources can be fairly large and spread out, and because it can be difficult to approach and hunt them undetected by deer, knowing how the buck accesses them is important. Once we locate his bedding area, we can determine these access routes by following faint trails and rub lines to the deer's lunch table. Not only is this much better than stabbing in the dark, but it also ups the odds of the deer passing within range of our weapon.

If our buck's typical midday activity involves traveling between two bedding areas, the faint trail connecting them is where we want to be. This setup allows us to slip between his beds, never crossing his trail, for a low-impact route. For the bowhunter, setting the stand approximately 15 yards on the downwind side of the trail and concealing it well all but ensures that his presence will be undetected. Because of that, the stand can be hunted repeatedly, with low odds of educating the mature buck.

Conclusion

Although morning hunting during the early, lull and post-rut/second-rut phases offers poor odds of harvesting a monster, midday and afternoon sits can be productive. When we hit the scraping phase, suddenly both morning and afternoon stands can produce equally well. Midday setups can then also be incorporated. This provides us the opportunity to break the hours of an all-day sit by hunting the first three hours in one stand, moving to one that covers trails between a buck's bedding areas and bedding/feeding areas, and then finishing off the day with a sit in one of our afternoon stands. Of course, any of the chasing and rut stages' stand sites are potential candidates for day-long sits as well.

Can a hunter shoot a buck of a lifetime at sunrise on opening day of archery season? Of course he can. As noted, mine are not hard-and-fast rules; they're the time slots and strategies I believe offer the greatest odds of a successful harvest, as well as the best odds of going undetected by deer. My approach to hunting deer is all about playing the odds, and the more we stack them in our favor, the more consistently successful we become.

PAT REEVE

The Perfect Tree

FIND ONE AND YOU'LL BE AHEAD OF THE GAME.

To this point, we've focused primarily on hunting strategies. Hopefully, we now have a fairly solid grasp of how we intend to attack each hunting season. Although we know that we still must remain flexible — there are, after all, exceptions to every rule — we now should be able to go to any new setting and, based on the phase of the season, know which areas are most likely to produce buck sightings. Once we locate such an area, if we intend to hunt from trees, the next step is finding the right one.

This step begs the question: What constitutes the perfect tree for hunting? As we'll discuss, the first trait is that it must be in a location we can get to and leave from without ruining our chances of success. That might sound like an easy enough task, but in many situations it can be quite challenging. Because of this challenge, along with the critical role that selecting the right tree plays in successfully tagging mature bucks, I've dedicated an entire chapter to this subject alone.

Playing The Wind

For hunters who aren't extremely odor-conscious, setting stands on the downwind side of their prey is critical. A whitetail's nose is by far its best weapon. As Dr. Karl Miller, a foremost expert on odor communications for the University of Georgia, once told me, we humans can't even begin to smell compared to deer. Whitetails rely on their ability to detect and decipher the odors they produce to communicate much like humans do with speech.

Simply put, deer are built to pick us off with their sense of smell. While conducting seminars, I often use the following example to illustrate this point. When I first walk into a fast-food restaurant, I smell frying burgers. A deer in the same situation would most likely smell burgers, buns, condiments, pickles, the cook's deodorant and a bevy of other smells, all at the same time. I believe that alone rules out relying on cover scents to fool a deer's sense of smell.

Another hurdle is that a whitetail's sense of smell is tied into the portion of its brain that's responsible for reflex reactions. When a deer sees something out of the ordinary, it often pauses to analyze it. However, when it catches an ample amount of odor associated with danger, its brain reacts, causing it to run, as opposed to "thinking" about what to do next. The deer's incredible sense of smell, its ability to differentiate numerous odors at once, and its reflex response all make getting past its nose a serious challenge.

One way of combating this is staying downwind of your prey. The majority of tree stands should be set to take advantage of the prevailing wind direction, with a few set to cover the other winds. That way, regardless of where a steady wind is coming from, the hunter has a stand that will work with it. Even when going to the odor-reducing extremes I do, I use that placement strategy. Then, if all else is equal, I sit the stands that are best for the wind.

Even if you're completely confident that you'll never get winded, prevailing wind directions should still factor into choosing the perfect tree. When setting up on any feature that bucks might be scent-checking, such as scrapes or family group bedding areas, the downwind side is the place to be. Not only will the animals at these specific locations be upwind of you, but you also will be in position to intercept many of the bucks scent-checking from a distance.

The same often holds true for feeding areas as well. When the cover and overall setting allow, bucks often approach from and/or parallel to the downwind side of the food source, allowing them to scent-check it for danger. During the rut, I've watched some of the more leery bucks check feeding does this way, as well. By employing this tactic, they don't have to expose themselves to potential danger needlessly. Instead, they remain hidden in the shadows unless they determine that a "hot" doe is out feeding.

As much as we've been told to let our odor blow into an open feeding area (as opposed to into the woods the deer presumably will be coming from), I've found that I've had more success being upwind of what I believe is a "dead zone" in the woods. This is the exact approach I take to hunting after the first rut, when even my own intense odor-reduction scheme can prove insufficient to keep me from getting busted. Not only does this approach allow for shots at bucks approaching or paralleling downwind,

Controlling your odor is a real plus for a deer hunter — especially in locations where the wind tends to shift frequently. Photo courtesy of Steve Bartylla.

but it also doesn't blow human odor to feeding deer. I doubt that anyone would argue with my belief that it's much easier to go undetected by deer passing downwind than it is to remain undetected by a group of deer camped out downwind. Because of that, along with the scent-checking aspect, I've always preferred the downwind side of feeding areas. Of course, if deer sign and sightings say otherwise, I'll try to take advantage of that, instead.

Finding The Distance

With our perfect tree being downwind of deer activity, the next question is, how far? The answer can, of course, vary dramatically, based on your weapon. Although I can consistently make shots of 200 to 300 yards with my rifle, I still strive for stand placements that put deer only 50 to 100 yards from me during gun season. That does two things for me. First, I find that range to be a gimme shot, often even when a deer is moving. Second, it keeps me at a distance at which I can still hide many of the common sins of stand-hunters, such as my movements and noises.

For bowhunting, 15- to 20-yard shots are ideal for me. Because I consistently practice out to 50 yards, assuming I don't mess up, accuracy in the 15- to 20-yard range isn't an issue. I also like the shot angle that distance presents from a tree. The closer the animal is at the time of the shot, the sharper the shot angle becomes, making it more difficult to achieve a double-lung hit.

This is a hard lesson I was taught in my early years. When I first began bowhunting, deer were few and far between in my area. That, combined with my hunting skills still being in the early developmental stage, resulted in my simply seeing a buck while bowhunting becoming an event to share with all of my friends. For the next week or two, you attained hero status through such a feat.

It's tempting to set up right on top of a hot trail, but that can lead to serious problems. Photo by Gordon Whittington.

Having seen a young forkhorn feeding on the opposite side of an alfalfa field two sits in a row was far more than I could resist. The next afternoon, armed with a saw, some boards, a handful of nails and a hammer, I made a stand on the trail he'd been using. Because the only tree suited for a permanent stand was literally right next to the trail, that's where I built my stand.

That afternoon, clad in a pair of jeans and a flannel shirt and clutching my 45-pound Shakespeare recurve, I waited for my first bow-killed buck to fall. Daydreaming as I watched the field, I didn't catch him coming until he was already within 10 yards of my tree. Luckily, I didn't have time to get nervous. Spinning in my stand, I drew and took the broadside 5-yard shot.

As the deer bounded off, the half of my fletchings still showing removed any doubt as to where I had hit. Tucked just behind the shoulder blade, a couple inches below the spine, the arrow was piercing his chest cavity.

I returned home to get my brother, Joe, and we were back tracking my trophy within the hour. The blood trail was good enough that even two boys in their early teens were able to follow it. Somewhere around 100 yards into the job, we jumped the buck the first time. Little did we know that we'd be repeating that event five or six times over the next 24 hours. The last time he waved goodbye with his flag, he'd shed the arrow and clotted up.

Although I didn't realize it until years later, the sharp shot angle had resulted in my arrow only catching a single lung. Unfortunately, such hits result in Vegas odds of a mortal shot. My yearling trophy survived to reach the age of 2 1/2, when an older friend harvested him during rifle season.

When you're hunting from an elevated position, bow shots of under 10 yards result in a much higher percentage of single-lung non-fatal hits. In addition to providing a better shot angle, setting up 15 to 20 yards from the trail or whatever other sign the bowhunter is covering also helps keep him out of the deer's direct line of sight. Obviously, this makes hiding movement easier. Furthermore, it's less likely that a deer will notice a blob of camo in a tree off to the side than one it's walking directly toward. All of these factors combined are why I strive to locate stands that provide shot opportunities at these ranges.

Bigger Is Better

Small-diameter trees make it much harder to blend in. Like so many other lessons in my whitetail career, I learned that one the hard way.

Once I got a few years of hunting experience under my belt, I decided it was time to start going after the big boys. Sure, I was naive to believe I was qualified at the time, but I had the youthful confidence that taking a handful of bow deer will bring.

Amazingly, I somehow was able to set up on a few decent bucks. One in particular appeared to be an easy mark. After seeing this very respectable buck do the same thing a handful of times, I devised a carefully crafted plan of attack. I'd go in and set up a stand on the trail I'd seen him using.

The only problem was that none of the trees in the area were very big. In hindsight, I should have constructed a small ground blind, but in those foolish days I believed you only shot deer from trees. So, I picked the only one that was marginally able to support my stand and slapped it in.

Hearing the approach of a trotting deer, I readied myself. Not long after the tree stopped swaying from my minimal movements, I saw him. The magnificent button buck was approaching at a full trot. Somewhere in the 30-yard range, he froze and stared a hole into the obscene growth that bulged malignantly from the small tree. After a couple of curious looks, the buck fawn tore off in the direction from which he'd come.

As hard as I tried to convince myself that taking the mature buck I was after was still possible from this stand, even at that age I knew that if I couldn't go undetected by a fawn that I would turn the big buck inside out. It was a humbling lesson to learn.

Looking back, I made more than a handful of mistakes in trying to take that gift-wrapped trophy buck. I spent over three hours disturbing and stinking up the woods, walking around and around in circles trying to find a tree that would work, only to clear the minimal cover it provided. Being as close to his bedding area as I was, those actions were the kiss of death by themselves.

Needless to say, even if I hadn't driven him into the next county with my disturbances, the buck fawn, as well as several other deer I saw on subsequent sits — I may have been ignorant, but at least I was persistent — all illustrated what his reaction would have been: to turn inside out and run for his life! By the way, the next time I saw that big buck was during firearms season, as he lay in the bed of my neighbor's pickup truck.

The moral of this painfully told story is that small-diameter trees are not a stand-hunter's friends. Within reason, the larger the tree's diameter, the better job it does of allowing the hunter to become one with the trunk. This alone can do a good job of breaking up the hunter's outline.

Seeking Cover

Of course, a mat of branches sure doesn't hurt, either. The setting of the deer's eyes in its head provides it with good peripheral vision, though at the cost of depth perception. A whitetail just isn't that good at picking up a motionless object that's behind, in front of, or in the middle of a mat of limbs, twigs and/or leaves.

Ideally, a large-diameter tree can be found that provides you with good front, back and side cover. With that, just enough branches can be trimmed to allow for shooting windows, and you'll be all but visually undetectable by deer. A hunter in this setup rarely gets seen, even if he moves at the wrong time.

Obviously, trees that provide all of this are rarely found in exactly the right place. When only given the choice of one, I'll go for back cover every time. I believe a backdrop does much more to break a silhouette than does frontal cover. Not only that, it also provides a background to help camouflage movement, as well as allowing for unobstructed shots in front of the hunter.

Another valuable form of cover is large branches shooting out below the stand. When thinking of cover, always consider the line of sight a deer will have to the stand. A large branch or two jutting out below the stand helps break up that view. Furthermore, it makes the stand and hunter more "natural" in appearance.

Lurking In Shadows

As the old saying goes, dangerous things lurk in dark places. Placing stands in the shadows is the icing on our perfect-tree cake.

This provides several benefits to the stand-hunter. First, we're much harder to pick out when tucked into the shadows. Second, not only are our outlines masked better by darkness, but our equipment also won't betray us as easily, either. Without the aid of direct sunlight, shiny surfaces — binocular lenses, broadheads, whatever — are nowhere near as obvious.

Granted, we should inspect and treat all of our equipment for potential glares. However, stands weather, and painted surfaces of other objects can chip when being transported. Then there's the pesky fact that we are only human and can miss things, along with the occasional tendency to take shortcuts. Placing stands in the shadows can help minimize the risk of shining a warning beacon into the eyes of an approaching monarch.

Lastly, being in the shade improves a hunter's own ability to see what's going on around his stand. It's much more effective to look out into better-lit areas than to peer from the brightness into darkness. As much as this is true for picking up the movement of game, it's even more important when trying to shoot under these conditions. In gun hunting, scopes tend to have the light-gathering power to make this more manageable.

This bowhunter has cover in front of and behind him. If you must choose between the two, it's better to go with the latter. Photo by Michael Skinner.

Bowhunters using peeps, though, can have extreme difficulties picking up the target under these conditions. Furthermore, regardless of the weapon, keeping the sun out of your eyes makes all of this much easier.

Reaching For Heights

How high a stand should be placed is one of the more common topics of debate among whitetail hunters. As with nearly every other great debate, both sides make valid points. The higher the stand is, the worse the shot angle can be, the more obstructions a bowhunter might have to shoot through, and the more dangerous it can be. Lower stands can make it easier for the deer to wind the hunter or see him, but such stands also can provide better angles and make tight tree-stand shooting form less of an issue.

Personally, I like my stands to be an honest 18 to 25 feet off the ground. That's where I'm most comfortable and confident. The precise height depends on where I can best take advantage of cover and where my stand will fit onto the tree. However, when hunting slopes or a tree that lacks cover, I'll go higher. If the only good tree provides the best cover at 10 feet, that's where my stand will go. For gun hunting, I'll go as high as needed to get the best combination of visual range and unobstructed shooting. The point is that I do have an ideal, but I remain flexible to adapt to the situation. I feel that taking this approach benefits me the most.

Regardless of the height you covet, the ideal tree should provide adequate cover at that level. If it doesn't, it's advised that you strongly consider altering your height standard. As more than one story in this chapter illustrates, it does little good to be in the right spot if your stand doesn't allow for a killing shot.

Conclusion

Finding the perfect tree makes success much more easily attained. Wind direction, shot distance, tree size, available cover, light angle and stand height all factor into this decision. Some items, such as wind direction, shot distance and tree size, are more critical than others. However, together, they all play important roles in creating the ideal tree in which to hang a stand.

Making It Work

TOM EVANS

Making It Work

IF A GREAT STAND SITE HAS NO IDEAL TREE, IMPROVISE.

It was the mother of all scrapes. The pawed area was the size of a kitchen table, the dirt still moist and pungent from having been repeatedly worked. Scattered about were coffee-can-sized trees shredded by antlers. I had the ideal route for a low-impact downwind entry. Everything was perfect, except for one pesky issue: The specific area in which I needed to put my stand didn't boast a single suitable tree. I finally walked away frustrated, believing I couldn't hunt such an area.

Probably more than anything else, my experiences as a trapper finally opened my eyes to how foolish this mindset was. In trapping, rarely is an area perfect for a set. Back in my early teens, I noticed that with a creative approach I could almost always work in an effective set, many times in areas other trappers simply wrote off as impossible. It eventually dawned on me that I could come up with non-standard ways of making deer stands work, as well.

Today some of these ways are not overly foreign, though most are still under-utilized. But back in those days, the handful of bowhunters I knew all hunted from homemade or portable tree stands, period.

In later years, I would learn that some visionary individuals, such as Gene and Barry Wensel, had been employing far more creative tactics well before the idea ever dawned on me. Still, it was when I decided to become more creative in my problem-solving skills that doors began opening. I no longer walk away from spots believing that I just can't get a stand in there. Instead, I find a way to make it work.

A hunter silhouetted against the sky makes for a nice photo — but setting up in this fashion is generally a one-way ticket to failure. Photo by Ron Sinfelt.

Creating Cover

In many situations, it isn't that there's a lack of trees able to support a stand. It's more often that those trees resemble telephone poles, owing to their lack of cover at or below stand height. As stated in the last chapter, that type of tree just doesn't work for bowhunting, and it's also far less than ideal for hunting with firearms.

So why don't we just add the cover we need? One way is as simple as cutting fresh branches and attaching them to the stand and/or tree. Of course, this can only be done on land where it's legal to do so; on many public lands there are strict rules against cutting branches or otherwise harming trees. However, in these settings, finding fallen branches and attaching them to the stand is still an option. You certainly can't nail materials to the tree, but you might be able to use wire, rope or a bungee cord to fasten some extra cover to it. Obviously, this approach also works on private land where the owner frowns on cutting or nailing into trees.

When selecting branches, keep in mind that some tree species hold their leaves longer than others. Poplars aren't a good choice, but most evergreens and oaks retain their foliage surprisingly

Adding cover can help you hide an otherwise exposed stand from a deer's sharp eyes. Photo courtesy of Steve Bartylla.

well. As with finding natural cover, the goal is to add enough cover to break us up and mask movement but still let us shoot effectively.

Another option is to attach camouflage screening behind your stand. This is a tactic my brother, Joe, has used often over the years. The advantage is that the netting never loses its leaves, it's quicker to put up, and it can be attached without anything being harmed. On the flip side, it creates a barrier that can't be shot through, and it can flutter unnaturally in the wind.

My preferred method of increasing cover is to enlist the aid of commercial tools. In today's hunting marketplace, there's a wealth of quality products geared for anything imaginable, including stand concealment. Of those I've tried, The Cover System is the one I like most and continue to use. It's simply a set of flexible branches that strap to the back of the tree or front of the stand. Once the unit is in place, it can be molded into any position that suits the hunter's needs. Just like that, the straightest telephone-pole-like tree provides instant cover. The Cover System is quick, easy and effective. No wonder it has swiftly become one of my most indispensable tree stand accessories.

Regardless of what's used to add needed cover, there's no longer a reason to walk away from trees large enough to safely hold a stand. The key is having the cover to break your outline. If we think creatively, we'll come up with the tools to modify a tree to the point that it works.

Size Matters

Although we can compensate for the diameter of a tree to a certain extent by introducing natural and/or artificial cover, there comes a point where it's just too small. The rule of thumb I use is simple: If the tree will sway from my own slow and careful movements, it just isn't going to work for hunting.

For one thing, there are more days with wind than not. If a stand is going to

Tower and tripod stands of various designs are becoming popular in many areas — especially where there is a shortage of stand-sized trees. Photo by Gordon Whittington.

bob around like a bobber in the ocean, there's no way to get off an ethical shot, no matter which weapon is being used. More importantly, there's the safety factor. It's simply much more difficult to maintain your balance on a swaying object. Finally, even if none of this mattered, the tree would likely give away your position as you ready yourself for the shot.

Outside of putting up support beams, there are options that will work. One of them is a ladder stand. Certainly, these also have a limit as to how small a tree can be used; however, braces at the midway point and in the platform area help to stabilize the stand, allowing for it to be used safely on smaller-diameter trees.

Along with that, once set up, ladders are easier to get into and out of than most climbers and hang-on stands. Because so many hunters enjoy this feature, as well as the overall comfort of ladder stands, more and more outfitters are switching to them. With clients possessing such a wide range of experience and physical abilities, ladders serve as a happy medium.

The downside to ladders — as well as climbers, for that matter — is that the trees on which they work best have limited cover at or below stand height. Luckily, the same methods of introducing artificial cover also work with ladders and climbing stands. With that, we take away one of the biggest problems historically experienced with both.

When the trees are too small even for a ladder, tripods provide a potential solution. Although most are designed more with the firearms hunter in mind, almost every Texas bowhunter I know has taken deer while perched in one. Again, among the greatest concerns I have when using them is cover. However, utilizing the previously mentioned techniques and putting a tripod in place well before its intended time of use make them much more effective. (As hard as it might be to believe, I know bowhunters who have taken mature deer while hunting from tripods set in the middle of areas devoid of cover at stand height. However, in that setting, I'd opt for a ground blind.)

Ground Blinds

I truly believe that ground blinds are among the most underutilized tools in the bowhunter's arsenal. For whatever reason, this is particularly true for those who bowhunt in the North and Upper Midwest. However, firearms hunters everywhere, along with bowhunters in the South and West, have long hunted at ground level and realize the benefits that strategy provides.

A ground blind can consist of nothing more than hunkering down behind natural cover, positioning a few branches for cover or using the quick, easy and incredibly effective popup blind. One technique I use combines both scouting and hunting from natural blinds of sorts. When an in-season scouting trip is needed, I often slowly scout through the woods. Upon finding a promising spot, I'll begin looking for a place in which to hunker down, such as a fallen tree. Snuggling into

POPUP BLINDS

Here are the features to look for when selecting a popup blind:

Open camouflage pattern: With larger blobs and contrasting colors, the pattern doesn't merge into one solid object.

Black interior: This hides hunter movement to the point that it's almost a non-issue.

Adequate size: No matter how big a blind you think you need, get it bigger. Moving around and shooting require plenty of space.

Easy setup and takedown: The blind will often be set up or taken down in the dark, so get one that is simple to use.

Large, numerous shooting windows: A blind with 360-degree windows minimizes the problem of being able to see well.

Window flaps: When the blind is set up so that deer can only approach from certain directions, closing the windows on the other side(s) masks your movement even more.

Quality craftsmanship: It pays to buy tools you can depend on.

the branches often provides all the cover you need.

The best ground-level locations are often on the trails between food sources and bedding areas. Here, deer are meandering through and generally are not in an ultra-alert state. That goes a long way toward counteracting the disadvantages of hunting on the ground.

I believe that the farther in advance a ground blind is constructed or set up, the better off a hunter will be. Because most, if not all, of the materials are natural, once any disturbances made during construction are gone and the deer have become accustomed to this new "brushpile," it will be widely accepted by the herd.

Among the biggest considerations when constructing these beauties is making sure you have ample room for positioning and firing the weapon. After that, the greatest trick is to only move when the deer is looking away. Finally, if the blind will be hunted within weeks of its being built, making it blend in with its surroundings is helpful. In short, follow these simple guidelines, along with the same placement strategies used for tree stands, and you'll increase the effectiveness of your ground blinds dramatically.

Popup blinds also fit nicely with the same placement strategies used for tree stands, but they have their own unique idiosyncrasies. It begins with the purchase. Look for the features in the accompanying chart and you really can't go wrong.

With that out of the way, let's look at some tricks that can increase a popup blind's effectiveness. For one, when a popup blind is used for bowhunting, archers using fixed-blade broadheads can cover the windows of the blind with shoot-through mesh. (Having practiced with mesh, I can say that I've never seen a loss of accuracy; still, I advise taking some practice shots before using one on a hunt.) The benefit of using mesh is that it eliminates the unnatural black holes seen in uncovered windows. (For blinds without black interiors, the open windows appear equally unnatural.)

When you're using an expandable-head arrow or a firearm, the windows should be left uncovered. In that case, it's best to try to break up the window's outlines with a few twigs and leaves. However, care must be used so those objects don't deflect the shot.

Another consideration for shooting from enclosed blinds is that the interior gets darker earlier in the evening and brightens later in the morning. To get the maximum legal shooting hours per day, Truglo's light-gathering pins and iron-sight attachments are recommended. Those who shoot scopes are typically unaffected.

Then we come to what to wear inside the blind. As odd as it might seem at first thought, black hoods, tops and pants are very good choices. Because of the black interior, being dressed from head to toe in black turns you into the "invisible man."

Finally, there's the question of placement. As with naturally constructed blinds, if popup blinds are put out several weeks before the first hunt, they can be set anywhere. Given this amount of time for deer to grow accustomed to them, it really doesn't matter how they are positioned or blended in.

When a popup blind is set up for an immediate hunt, certain guidelines have proven to me to be the best. First, popups startle deer most often when they surprise them at close distances. For example, a deer is walking a trail in the woods, rounds a tree, and suddenly sees the blind at 30 yards or closer. The result is seldom good. When a popup is used either in the woods or in areas where deer cannot see it from a distance of 50 yards or farther, the best results will be found from brushing in the blind well with natural cover or the same Cover System branches recommended for use with tree stands.

Field edges are about the most troublesome spots I've found for popups. Because deer are naturally on ultra-alert when approaching fields, they are far more likely to notice a brushed-in blind there. The solution to this is placing the blind right out in the middle of the field, doing nothing to conceal it. Sure, it sticks out like a sore thumb, but so does a large round hay bale left by a farmer. With the deer being able to see the blind from a distance, they have ample time to analyze it and categorize it as harmless. At that point, even the majority of those touchy old does brush it off as nothing to be concerned about. (If you doubt this claim, ask yourself how many times you've heard of deer blowing at fresh round hay bales. Also, think of how often deer prove willing to feed upwind of trucks parked in the middle of fields.)

The advantages popups provide are many. In less than a minute (often under five even when brushing is required), they can be up and ready to hunt from, regardless of the habitat. They're quick and easy and open the door to effectively hunt nearly any setting. For those who have a bias against hunting from the ground, I recommend that you seriously reconsider. I know I was glad when I finally did.

Conclusion

Regardless of whether it's done by improving trees, using various stand types, or hunting from the ground, there's really no reason for the lack of a perfect tree to keep a whitetail hunter from setting up in any location. When you approach such a challenge with the right attitude and a little creative thinking, you can make it work. Doing so provides you with an advantage over many other hunters. I don't know about you, but I'll take every ethical advantage I can get.

STEVE BARTYLLA

Shooting Lanes

TO CUT OR NOT TO CUT: THAT REALLY IS THE QUESTION.

I believed that I'd taken a negative and transformed it into a positive. Upon my arrival at northwestern Missouri's Bucks and Beards Outfitters, owner Donnie McClellan had given me some bad news: The lease I'd hunted the last three years was no longer his. Because I always do my own scouting and stand preparation, that meant I'd have to start from scratch. My expectations went from being very confident that I'd leave with a nice buck to knowing I had my work cut out for me. Luckily,

I also knew that Donnie still controlled the best land in the area and that he always kept pressure amazingly low.

Being as gracious as he is, my host's first offer was to put me up in one of the many stands he already had in position for his clients. Because we are friends, and Donnie knew that the thrill for me lies in pulling things together for myself, he wasn't surprised when I politely declined the offer. That's when Donnie pulled out the aerial photos of a new farm he'd just acquired.

With only five days to hunt, I did the unheard of. Despite my cameraman's protests that we needed to get into a tree, I invested the majority of the first three days scouting to find the two best stand sites for the last two days of my hunt. Because of the vast acreage the farm covered, I needed all three days for foot scouting and observations. Over the years, I have developed the philosophy that it's far better to spend less time in the very best stands than to spend more in marginal setups. Finally confident that I'd found the best spots, I set out to hang a couple of stands.

Because the chase phase was now in full swing, both spots selected were along the edge of cedar thickets that served as bedding areas. The first was a square-shaped thicket with a wooded dry run connecting the southwest corner to another large body of woods. From the dry run, a sharp cut ran along the thicket, funneling most of the deer wanting to enter the thicket through a low spot in the run. That's where I chose to hang my first stand.

The other location was rather similar: a huge, nasty cedar thicket that gradually opened to mature woods as it neared a small stream. The stream itself eventually became the edge of a fencerow when it left the woods and sliced through a soybean field. From one spot between the cedar thicket and stream, a hunter on stand could cover movement along the stream, the deer piling out of the thicket to feed, and the best trails running from the mature woods into the thicket. With both stands being on the downwind side of the thickets, I felt pretty good about them.

Having showered, dressed in Scent-Lok and sprayed down well with Scent Killer, I headed out at midday and set the stands as quietly as possible, trimming as little as I could and still have some hope that one of my windows would provide a shot. Of the two stands, the one along the stream presented the bigger challenge in that regard. With my being in the transition area where the thicket begrudgingly became mature woods, natural openings were few and far between. To compensate, I relied exclusively on the clippers to create three 2-foot-wide windows: one toward the thicket, another toward the field, and the last toward the stream. Feeling fairly certain that anything coming from behind me would only provide a head-on shot anyway, I left that area alone. After clipping the branches, which produces less odor than sawing, I removed each and stashed them a safe distance away. I knew that the success of this

How many shooting lanes to cut, and how large to make them, will vary from setup to setup. Ron Willmore chose not to clear much around his Illinois tree stand, and as a result had to make a tricky shot as this buck walked through a tiny hole in thick brush. Often the hunter isn't as happy with the results of such a shot. Photo by Gordon Whittington.

stand would depend on keeping the disturbances from this level of work to an extreme minimum.

Because the other stand covering the cut crossing point required fewer disturbances, I sat it first to provide an extra day's rest for the stream stand. Light had no more than begun to take over when I caught the movement of a buck heading toward me. Just as I had hoped, he was making his way along the cut to cross into the thicket and check the breeding status of the does it held. At around 50 yards, the clean 10-point rack with respectable mass and tine length convinced me that this buck was in the "shooter" category.

Shooting Lanes

I could see that the deer was going to provide me with a gimme 15-yard shot. As I drew my bow, I already had him on the wall. Bending at the waist, I tucked my pin neatly behind his shoulder and smoothly squeezed off the shot.

My eyes stared in disbelief as the buck ran away, my arrow sticking out of his neck. I refused to believe it. Whether practicing or shooting at game, I always know at the moment I squeeze off the release or trigger if I've made a good shot. That was a good shot, and I was 100 percent confident of it. So, how could I have missed my aiming point by *three feet*?

After the buck disappeared, I thoroughly went over the events in my mind. I'd inspected my equipment as I always do upon getting into my stand, remained calm for the shot, used proper shooting form, picked my spot and smoothly triggered the release. That buck should have toppled before cresting the deep cut, and certainly he shouldn't have been hit where the arrow struck.

That's when I noticed the small twig, now precariously dangling from a thread of bark. I'd broken my own golden rule: I'd left an obstruction in one of my shooting windows.

Certainly, even when prepping a stand for an immediate hunt, you must minimize the amount of trimming you do. But it never fails that if one twig is left in your shooting window, your arrow will find it.

Certainly, even when prepping a stand for an immediate hunt, you must minimize the amount of trimming you do. But it never fails that if one twig is left in your shooting window, your arrow will find it. That's exactly what had happened to me. Frankly, I knew better. I just somehow missed seeing it. If I had, it would have been trimmed . . . and that lost buck would now be on my wall instead.

As it turned out, the arrow deflected and hit the dead zone between the deer's spine and windpipe. I found the arrow approximately 100 yards away, and the blood trail dried up shortly after. After the last speck of blood was found, the buck had lost less than 8 fluid ounces. I knew he would suffer nothing more than a pain in the neck, but I spent the rest of the day combing the thicket all the same. It had been a long time since I had last hit an animal that wasn't successfully recovered, and I really wanted to keep that streak alive. More importantly, I owed it to the animal to be 200 percent certain that I either retrieved him or he survived.

The next morning found me in the stream stand. A little after first light, an old doe and her fawns meandered through two of my shooting lanes, making their way from the beans to the safety of their daytime bedding thicket. As the doe calmly passed through my shooting lanes, I felt good about the caution I had exercised in cutting them.

A half-hour after first light, I drew the grunt tube to my mouth and began an elaborate sequence. Beginning with three estrous-doe calls, I switched over to a tending grunt and then alternated the tone between grunts. After one more hard grunt, I removed the tube and did my best snort-wheeze. With my head on a swivel, looking for an approaching buck, I snatched the rattling antlers and created my best 20-second brawl, ending with another doe call and a series of grunts. My goal was to paint the picture of a "hot" doe, two bucks chasing her and eventually fighting to win her favor, with the victor resuming his pursuit.

Apparently it worked. At the sound of a snapping twig behind me, I carefully turned to see a truly spectacular buck approaching. His massive main beams spread somewhere well beyond 25 inches, and each sported five typical points. His obscenely long tines seemed to jut stickers and kickers everywhere. This buck easily would score over 200 inches, making Boone as either as a typical or a non-typical. He was glorious . . . and he was coming in on a rope.

Knowing there was no way to shoot the deer while he was behind me, I continued to look forward and remain motionless, waiting for the big deer to reach my stand. I honestly don't get shaken easily while hunting, but I have to admit that not being able to watch what this giant was doing got to me. After less than two minutes that seemed more like two lifetimes, he was within inches of the base of my tree.

As the buck stood there, searching hard for the players in my little show, the sight of him allowed me to gather myself again and switch into predator mode. The hawthorn tree I was in was engulfed by an Osage orange tree. Because of the thick mat of branches, I'd have to wait until the buck stepped out to at least the 10-mark before I could take a shot.

Slowly the monster worked out to nine yards, then stopped again and scanned the area. One more yard and he'd be in my lane. Drawing as he stepped, I realized that all I needed now was for him to turn. Two, four, eight more steps, and he was still walking straight away. At 20 yards he stopped again, slowly looking from side to side, trying to find his doe. Five more yards and he'd be into the thicket and out of my life.

As the buck took another step, I grunted with my mouth, desperately trying to get him to turn. Looking over his shoulder, he flicked his tail, as if to say, "I didn't get this old by being that stupid. I was just standing there, and I know there isn't a deer here." The buck gave one more casual flick of his tail, and the thicket swallowed him.

I tried calling him back several more times that day, but it just wasn't to be. Still, I chalked it up as a very successful day. I'd managed to hang a stand two days before, clear far more brush than I was comfortable with, and still had duped an incredible buck, even as he brushed against my tree steps, into believing I had never set foot there. To me, that made for a very good day in the woods.

In-Season Clearing

The reason I invested so much space in this chapter to those two hunts is that I believe they illustrate many solid points. Both show the delicate balance that must be struck between doing too much clearing and not doing enough. In both cases, the oblivious nature of the bucks clearly showed that I hadn't gone overboard. Truth be told, slipping my trimming past that old doe was even more impressive.

When prepping stands to be hunted within days, low impact is the key. Not only should these activities be conducted during midday hours, when deer are least active, and scent reduction be taken to the extreme, but the trimming we do must also be minimized. Twenty years ago, I'd have cleared massive lanes and either not seen a single deer or had them bolt as soon as they neared the opening. Today, I'm a firm believer that less is more, particularly when the stand will be hunted soon thereafter.

Of course, even under those conditions, I have a limit to how little I'll do. Ideally, I want a lane two to three feet wide to my front, as well as one to each side and a fourth behind me. When I don't believe I have a legitimate chance at a shot in one direction, I'm willing to leave that side alone, in an attempt to further minimize my disturbance. However, every single obstruction must be removed from the windows I cut. If not, it seems that my arrow, or bullet for that matter, will find one every time. Taking this approach, along with extreme odor reduction and proper timing for the activity, has allowed me to successfully hunt stands the very day they were hung.

Pre-Season Clearing

When preparing stands well before hunting, the rules change. Although I still don't make massive shooting lanes, I'm more liberal with the clearing I do. The approach that works best for me is to create numerous narrow windows, as opposed to a few really wide ones. The narrow windows look more natural, and because of that, deer dismiss them as harmless well before hunting season begins.

As with clearing during hunting season, I strive to have lanes 2 to 3 feet wide in front, to the sides and behind me. Taking it even further, I also create windows 5 to 10 yards from the point at which I expect the shot to occur on either side of the main lanes. I look at these as windows of second opportunity. For example, if a buck is walking down a trail, he'll now pass through three lanes. The first probably won't offer a good chance when bowhunting, because of a slightly quartering-to-me angle. However, 5 to 10 yards farther, he'll reach the main window. If for whatever reason a shot doesn't occur at that point, the deer continues 5 to 10 yards to the third lane. Taking this approach typically results in at least two opportunities to shoot any deer traveling within range. Envision the lanes radiating out from the stand much like the spokes of an old wagon wheel.

I'm certainly not the only one to appreciate the value of numerous shooting windows. Successful trophy hunter and good friend Jim Hill also places a premium on having multiple options.

"I pay careful attention to trimming shooting lanes," says Jim. "If anything, I trim a little too much. I can fool a deer by not moving at the wrong time, but it's too late when I'm sitting on a stand

A "pole" trimmer is especially handy for clearing shooting lanes around your tree stands. Photo courtesy of Steve Bartylla.

and find I don't have an opening to take a shot or my arrow is deflecting off a branch. Of course, any serious trimming needs to be done well before the season. The way I look at it, with anything I can control, if I take a chance, that can be the one time I blow it. It's easy to fall into the trap of taking shortcuts, but they will eventually be costly.

"Taking these extra steps has been important in taking more than a couple of my best bucks," my friend says. "Just a few years ago, it was key. When I went to hang a stand in July, it was hot and all the leaves were out, but I kept looking until I came up with the tree I wanted. When I finally got the stand up, I rehearsed the possible shots. I just wasn't happy with shooting behind me. There was a dead tree that was going to get in my way if something sneaked in back there. I could get around it, but I didn't like it. I spent over 20 minutes cutting a large notch in the dead tree so I could get an easy shot in that direction. I'm glad I did! The buck I shot that year came in fast from behind me. If I hadn't spent the time on that branch, I don't think I ever would have got him."

Conclusion

As Jim's buck illustrates, putting in the extra effort to create ample shot opportunities can easily make the difference between a filled tag and a close call. Regardless of whether shooting lanes are created during or well before hunting season, the key is making them appear natural. During the season, seemingly little things, such as taking care with timing, being careful with odor control, using a pruner, removing the clipped branches, and keeping lanes to a reasonable minimum, all go a long ways toward keeping deer blissfully unaware. Finding the fine balance between that and having ample shooting widows is the art behind trimming lanes. And the better we hone our artist skills, the more rewards we'll reap.

Stand Adjustments

MIKE CLERKIN

Stand Adjustments

WHEN SHOULD YOU MOVE? WHERE SHOULD YOU GO?

It was one of the most bizarre occurrences I'd ever witnessed while hunting. I'd filled my Wisconsin buck tag and was heading north on a doe hunt to be covered for the bowhunting.net Web site. Having been on this late-season hunt many times before, I was confident enough to promise the editor and Webmaster that it would be an easy one, to be followed by a lot of photos of our group of three posing with our does. Little did I know that filling a tag would be a significant challenge.

Stand Adjustments

The approach to late-season hunting in this setting is simple: All you must do is find the hottest food source — typically consisting of recent logging activity or young regrowth — then find the best trail, set up where you can remain undetected and watch the parade of deer saunter by. It's as simple as one, two, three. That is, unless it's the first year the DNR has allowed three separate rifle seasons, two of them geared exclusively toward thinning the doe population. The deer that remained were more skittish than any I'd ever hunted.

I located an area where heavy winds had toppled a stand of poplars, and the deer sign indicated heavy feeding activity on the blown-down trees. Taking advantage of the virtual whitetail smorgasbord of tender buds, I set a stand along one of the well-used trails running from the heavy cover. I then sat there the first afternoon and saw nothing.

The second was more eventful, but no less frustrating. Twenty minutes after I climbed into my stand, a nubbin buck browsed his way through. Slipping out of my Heater Body Suit, I got ready. Sure enough, within five minutes a mature doe began coming toward me on the same path. Slowly turning, I did no more than brush the tree I was in, making such a soft noise I barely even heard it . . . and she bolted without hesitation.

It wasn't until the final 10 minutes of light that I saw another doe cautiously making her way into range. In the thick pines off to one side, I caught the movement of yet another doe also carefully slipping toward me. Behind her was a third mature doe. To say this one was responding with extreme caution would be a tremendous understatement. She'd take one step, stop and wait and wait and wait, check the wind, look in every possible location and finally take another cautious step.

As the lead doe neared my shooting lane, I began to draw. I'd taken extreme steps to ensure my equipment was as silent as possible, particularly so for this late-season hunting. Still, the softest whisper my carbon arrow made as I pulled it over my felt-covered rest was enough to tip her off; she was gone in a flash. Never in my life had I seen deer anywhere near this jumpy. The three rifle seasons they had endured had transformed them into ultimate survivors.

Because I'd managed to spook every doe I'd seen to this point, I knew that if I wanted any realistic chance of filling my tag, I'd have to relocate my stand or spend my last afternoon of bow season watching tails once again. Some would think changing stands foolhardy for the final day of the season, but I saw it as my only option for ending it with a successful harvest.

With this in mind, I selected the next-best trail leading from cover to browse. Because of the disturbance of hanging a stand, I tried to put it just far enough away so I could get it up without the bedded deer hearing me. I also did almost no clearing of shooting lanes.

I managed to pull it off just in time. I'd no more than settled in when I caught movement emerging from the pines. Luckily, I saw the deer at the first possible opportunity and had plenty of time to position myself. The young doe didn't have any fawns, so I'd only have to contend with her. After carefully getting into position, I readied myself. I knew all too well that these deer redefined the term "skittish," so I decided to draw while the doe was as far out as I could reasonably hold. Even then, I half-expected her to bolt.

Holding until the doe reached a broadside position seemed to take an eternity. Steadying myself, I placed my pin behind her shoulder. Squeezing off the shot, I knew it was true; the doe ran a mere 60 yards before toppling.

I'm sure most of you are thinking this successful doe hunt wasn't a big deal. However, based on the skittishness of the animals I was chasing, to say I was thrilled is an understatement.

Making The Move

While that story didn't end with me holding up an incredible rack, it does make a point: I never shy away from adjusting my strategy and/or stand placement, even when there's only one day of season left and my only hope is to fill a doe tag. When things aren't working out, change what you're doing.

One of the most common ways to make adjustments is shifting a particular stand to cover deer movement better. I've always viewed sitting a stand as one

A single sighting in the "wrong" place can be a random event — but if you see one or more bucks in that location a second time, don't wave it off as mere coincidence. The deer are trying to tell you something. Photo by Ron Sinfelt.

part hunting and one part scouting. Certainly, I do what I can to get my stand positioned right the first time. Still, sometimes I miss. If I observe a shooter buck repeating a pattern more than once outside of my effective weapon range, I react. Taking the same precautions outlined regarding setting stands for immediate use, I'll relocate my stand.

Although I never shift on the basis of just one observation, I'll almost always apply the two-strike rule, even from one season to the next. And this is the case no matter how "wrong" it might seem to be. It was a lesson I had to learn the hard way.

Having found a narrow strip of woods slicing between a heavily grazed cow pasture and a picked soybean field that nicely connected two large chunks of woods, I was confident that I had a killer stand location that would work well for both the chase and breeding phases of the rut. Yes, there was a heavily used trail crossing the cow pasture, but the funnel was the obvious spot for a trophy whitetail to cross. What self-respecting mature buck would stroll across the cow pasture in broad daylight, when an easily traveled funnel was so close by?

There are settings in which bucks move through a general area, but rarely on the same path twice. One time it might be here, another there and yet another somewhere new.

After failing to call into range several mature bucks I saw crossing the cow pasture, I finally moved the stand. It was too late for that year, but the outfitter I was helping has had clients take bucks from the cow pasture trail every year since. When it comes to a buck's prowling patterns through an area, unless major habitat changes occur, they have a very strong tendency to repeat the same patterns each time they pass through an area.

The same often holds true for other bucks, as well. In the case of the pasture, there was a reason the bucks crossed where they did: It was the quickest way to get from point A to point B. Granted, the funnel was barely out of the way and provided superior cover, but due to the lack of hunting pressure, the local bucks evidently felt safe enough to cross. Due in large part to a great entry and exit route existing to the stand, they still do to this day. Simply put, when a specific shooter or two different shooters are seen traveling through the same area in the same way twice, I adjust my stand placement to take advantage of it, whether it's for that season or seasons to come.

One obvious exception comes to mind. There are settings in which bucks move through a general area, but rarely on the same path twice. One time it might be here, another there and yet another somewhere new. If it proves to be just plain impossible to find or create a feature that narrows down the buck traffic, moving stands based on the two-occurrence guideline can drive a hunter mad. Instead, place a stand where it lets you cover the majority of the traffic— maybe even hang two stands for various wind directions — and depend on the law of averages to bring a buck into range.

Minor Adjustments

Another good reason to move a stand is because you got busted cold. Many hunters aren't overly concerned about being busted by does, because their goal is to tag a monster buck. Still, spooking does presents a twofold problem. First, does seldom leave quietly. After stomping and snorting for several minutes, they often retreat from the scene, blowing for five minutes or longer from a distance. Although it's debatable that this indeed ruins the entire sit, it certainly doesn't help. With does' tendency to bust a hunter repeatedly from the same stand, this can become more than a minor annoyance.

The other problem is that, the closer we are to either side of the rut, the odds of that doe leading a buck toward our stand are better than we'd care to admit. If and when she does, it rarely turns out well for the hunter. Once an old doe busts you, most often she'll be looking for trouble every time she comes through. It's been my experience that once she busts you twice in the same spot, it's end game.

When this occurs, a minor adjustment can put an end to the misery. All you must do is shift the position of the stand 20 yards or farther from its original position to begin fresh again. However, if the shift is less than 50 yards or so, it's especially important that the new stand site provide adequate cover. Does are often harder to chase off than bucks, but the older ones are also more observant. Their senses are on even more heightened alert as they travel through areas in which they've experienced danger. If the stand isn't concealed well, a doe is still likely to pick you off after a short-distance relocation.

Redefining The Game Plan

Another time when adjustments need to be made is when things just aren't falling into place and you aren't seeing the caliber of bucks you seek. I do as much of my scouting and stand prep as I can before the season. Frankly, spring is my crunch time. That's when I unravel most of the mysteries, analyze options and get most of my stands up for the lull, scraping, chase and rut phases of season. My early-season plan of attack is devised during late summer. When everything goes my way, the only time span I rely on in-season scouting to put me into position for is the secondary rut and/or post-rut. Otherwise, my plan is to have everything already in place for each phase of deer season before the archery opener.

That said, I can't remember a season in which I didn't have to reinvent the wheel in some manner. Sure, a lot of work and analysis go into finding honeyholes for each phase of the season, but there's still room for error. Unless you've hunted the same area for years, chances are that some of the stands won't be as good as you'd hoped. This is particularly true when you consider the dynamic changes that both the deer and habitat go through during the course of a season. To be right every single time is the goal we should all shoot for. However, only the most arrogant believe they won't make a mistake or two along the way. (We often learn much more from our errors than from our successes. That's why I've included in this book so many stories highlighting my own blunders.)

When you make a mistake on stand placement, don't live with it — fix it! In talking with other hunters at my seminars, I'm amazed at how many are willing to climb into the same, tired stands time after time after time after time when they either aren't seeing the deer they want or are getting busted by those they do see.

If a hunter truly has access to very limited acreage, and acquiring more honestly isn't an option, my heart bleeds for him. However, more often the hunter either believes things will just magically get better or he's just too lazy to make it happen. We'll throw out the lazy group because they seldom buy books to try to improve their skills and probably aren't in the audience. However, if you fall into the group who believe that the stand will get better "any day now," be aware that they usually don't. The one obvious exception is when you're hunting a stand site a season phase or two before you should. Even then, you're making that spot less productive by repeated hunting there before it's the stand's time to shine.

I once was in this group, so don't feel bad. In my youth, anytime I sat a stand without seeing a deer, I mistakenly believed my odds were improved for the next sit. After all, deer had to be using the trail, so it only stood to reason that they'd come through the next afternoon or the afternoon after that or the one after that. You know what? Far more often than not, I was wrong.

If you aren't seeing the caliber and/or number of deer you want, go out and find them. Invest an afternoon slowly stalking through the woods with the wind in your face. Drive around and glass food sources to see what's hot. Set up an observation post that provides a good view of a large area. In short, one way or another, find the deer you're after, then return the next midday to set up on them.

Conclusion

Regardless of whether it's tweaking stand locations to better cover movement, to avoid repeated bustings or because you just plain got it wrong the first time, living with bad breaks is a mistake. Dig a little deeper, and you'll find that consistently lucky hunters make their own luck. One of the ways they do it is by realizing when an adjustment needs to be made and then taking the initiative to make it.

MICHAEL SKINNER

Slip In, Slip Out

BECOME A SNEAK, OR YOU'LL LIKELY WISH YOU HAD.

I was set. For three afternoons in a row, two beautiful bucks had worked the same hot scrape flanking the edge of a narrow, hidden bean field. It had begun with a farmer telling me that he'd seen both bucks, seemingly oblivious of him, work the scrape as he'd been picking his beans. Because the field itself was shy of 10 acres, the farmer was rather astounded that the deer had calmly gone about their business, as if he wasn't even there.

At this point in my evolution as a hunter, I'd taken just

enough good bucks to know that this was a good thing, and I didn't want to mess it up. With the bean field being flanked by two towering, wooded ridges, I picked a vantage point that allowed me to survey the field without getting busted. Two afternoons in a row, I then watched the two bucks: first a heavy-beamed 8-pointer, trailed 20 minutes later by a great 10.

The next afternoon, a good three hours before I'd previously seen the 4x4 work through, found me slinking along the edge of the beans with a climber on my back. About 20 yards before I reached the stand tree I'd pegged from my observations on the ridge, a sudden crashing above me made my heart sink. Looking up, I saw the two bucks bounding away from the ridge finger they apparently shared. From their vantage point, they'd watched me walk most of the way in, holding fast until they deemed me a threat.

Needless to say, I didn't arrow either of those two beauties. In fact, my relative inexperience dealing with big boys resulted in several more foolish mistakes that led to my never seeing either of them again. Although I already knew the importance of entrance and exit routes, that afternoon was really the trigger I needed to begin addressing them with the respect that they demand.

The Critical Nature Of Undetected Travel

The importance of undetected routes should already be apparent to most readers. First, if you can't get to your stand without alerting deer, right off the bat you're at a disadvantage. Sure, an unsuspecting deer might later wander past, but more likely you already cooked your own goose on the way in. What's more, in and around the rut, spooking does is every bit as bad as spooking the buck. Although it's possible that a buck you bumped could still follow an unsuspecting doe past your stand, you can pretty safely bet that any spooked doe won't come back again soon.

Even during the non-rutting portions of deer season, spooking does is rarely a good thing. Their tendency to stomp and snort is rarely ever anything but detrimental. Furthermore, in terms of the early portions of the season, they'll likely be our buck bait later in the year. Although they're harder to push enough to make them abandon a portion of their home range, it's far from impossible. Of course, it isn't nearly that hard to make them more nocturnal. When a doe is paired up with a shooter buck, her daylight movement is our friend.

In the late season we aren't doing ourselves any favors, either. Sure, that doe has already been bred, but what about her doe fawn(s)? After the rut the family group comes back together, and the matriarch doe again sets the lead for her clan. If she's afraid to move, chances are pretty good that her doe fawn(s) won't be going anywhere, either.

As alluded to, bumping bucks during the rut isn't always the kiss of death. Because he's so strongly driven by his urge to breed, a buck will occasionally follow a "hot" doe right through a location in which he had a recent near-death experience. However, few hunters would argue that spooking rutting bucks isn't detrimental to our goal. Granted, I don't believe that spooking a buck once causes him to alter his long-term pattern, but I'll put my money on not seeing him again that day. I might lose that bet occasionally, but I'll get rich in the long run.

Repeated bumpings of bucks are a completely different story. Mature bucks are tough enough to hunt when they don't realize they're being chased. When they figure it out, the game gets exponentially harder. It doesn't take all that many brushes with hunters for an animal to figure out that it's being threatened. When that happens, more often than not, it typically results in the deer leading a more nocturnal lifestyle or making some other adjustment to its movement pattern.

Many deer hunters worry far more about the route to a stand than they do about the route away from it, particularly at day's end. But even if that day's hunting isn't affected by your exit route, you don't want to bump deer on the way out. If you intend to hunt the area again, whether you kick deer on the way in or the way out, you lose.

Finally, as it applies to all white-tails, ignorance is the hunter's bliss. Even when they move freely during

Keeping local deer unaware of you is always a plus — and it applies to does as much as to bucks. Photo by Ron Sinfelt.

daylight hours, deer that have repeated brushes with hunters are nervous. Their senses are keyed a level higher, they're more fidgety, and they're far more likely to run first and ask questions later. Simply put, nothing good comes from sloppy entrance and exit routes.

Using Terrain And Water Features

I find the need for stealthy entry and exit to be so important that I've spent hours dreaming of either constructing tunnel systems or having teleporting technology to get to and from my stands. Of course, teleportation isn't yet an option, and with the man-hours it would take to create tunnel systems being prohibitive, I've had to come up with other methods of getting in and out.

One of them is choosing paths that let me keep a low profile. Walking the bottoms of sharp cuts, drainage ditches or any other depressions helps to keep me out of sight. To further help matters, a pre-season trip can allow the hunter armed with clippers and saw to clear the path. This results in an easier and quieter route in. Provided this path is used when the wind won't carry your odor to otherwise unsuspecting deer, you have a good route.

The author approaches a stand via water. If you have this option, it can pay off handsomely. Photo courtesy of Steve Bartylla.

A further consideration is the need to stay off deer trails as much as possible. We don't have to concern ourselves only with odors drifting to deer as we travel; we also have to worry about the odors left behind. Deer can pick up human scent on a branch as long as two days after it was deposited. With deer typically traveling around sharp cuts, rather than through them, walking the bottom offers the advantage of not leaving clues after the fact. This is particularly true when the stand is situated alongside the cut. That scenario provides one of the best low-impact entrance and exit routes there are. All you must do is pop out to get into the stand and then drop back into the low area at hunt's end.

Traveling waterways offers the same key advantages. Provided you don't brush against overhanging branches, grasses, etc., moving via water allows you to avoid leaving any foreign odors behind. Furthermore, it provides a low-elevation and potentially quiet route. As is the case with stands set up along cuts, those along water features can be the ultimate for getting to and from a stand without being noticed by whitetails in the area.

When natural features aren't present to hide your travels, another option is relying on your knowledge of how deer use the local habitat. In its simplest form, the goal must be to avoid feeding areas on the way in for a morning hunt and to stay away from bedding areas on the way out in late morning, with the reverse being true for afternoon hunts. Still, because of the potential odors left behind, along with deer not always being where they're supposed to be, traveling areas completely void of deer is even better. Of course, that rarely translates into taking the straightest path between two points. When factoring in wind, sight and sound, going two, three, four or even more times out of the way is often needed.

Luckily, I've found two ways to slip through the woods without fear of having deer bust me on my trail. One is washing my rubber boots inside and out with Scent Killer liquid soap, spraying down with Scent Killer, and then using boot pads drenched in non-estrous doe urine. Another is spraying down a pair of Elimitrax overboots before heading through the woods. These overboots are made of a material that contains no odors and won't allow gasses to pass through. Provided that I don't touch anything with my bare skin, both approaches have worked flawlessly for me. Using either method, I've never seen a deer become alarmed when crossing my trail.

Going In At First Light

Another little thing that has helped me travel undetected is waiting for first light before heading to my stand in the morning. Don't get me wrong — if I have an easily traveled, low-impact route that provides little chance of bumping deer, I want to be in my stand a good half-hour or more before shooting could potentially occur. However, if it's dicey at all, I've come to believe that going in during gray light provides a greater advantage than getting in early.

Why? The simple answer is that I can see better. It's debatable either way whether flashlights spook deer. Personally, when I do use one it's a small Maglite I can cover with my thumb. When I feel I need to see something ahead of me, I move my thumb just enough to illuminate the spot. Even if I didn't cover the light, I'd never be able to walk through the woods in the dark as quietly as in the light.

Not only does gray light allow me to see where I'm going, but it also gives me a chance to see deer before they see me. In these situations, I often stalk my way in. When I catch the flicker of movement, I can choose to hold up long enough to allow the deer to pass, circle out around it, or try to position myself for a shot. In the dark, none of these is a viable option. Instead, I typically don't know they were there until I hear them crashing away, leaving me guessing as to the caliber of deer I just spooked.

As much as this timed approach helps for difficult routes through the woods, I find it even more helpful when I'm on a morning hunt near a field in which the deer are feeding. By having the ability to scan the field before entry, I can spot deer that might still be feeding or bedded in the food source. Once again, I can either choose to wait them out, determine a route that will allow me to reach the stand undetected, or try to put a sneak on them. I've found that this approach works so well that I rarely climb into a stand guarding a food source without gray light accompanying me. The alternative is far too often blowing deer out as I try to sneak along the field edge.

If your only morning entry route takes you through a field or pasture, it might help to hang back until gray light and then glass. Photo by Ron Sinfelt.

One exception to this is when I have a back door I can slip through to the stand. There are setups in which the woods provide a hunter a good approach from the back side of a stand guarding a food source. When such a route offers an undetectable approach from deer in the field, I'll gladly get in well before first light.

Another exception to using gray light for difficult entrances to both in-woods and field-edge stands is during the high-pressure days of firearms seasons. In that case, I always want to be in position at least an hour before first light. Yes, even though I'll be using the best entry route I can find, I still might bump deer on the way in before daylight. However, by being one of the first guys into the woods, I'll usually have enough other hunters coming in after me to reshuffle the cards back in my favor. In those situations, I always try to play it so they're moving deer toward me, not the other way around.

Using The "Buddy System"

In areas where tractor, truck and/or ATV traffic is common, these modes of transport can be very effectively used to help us get into and out of the woods. A great example of this is how Wisconsin outfitter Tom Indrebo gets many of his clients to and from their stands. With all of the work Tom does on ATVs throughout the year, the resident deer have become so tolerant of these vehicles that they dismiss them as harmless. That allows him to drive hunters directly to the stand. Amazingly, many of the trophy whitetails Tom's clients harvest watch the ATV drive past and back again, only to get up and walk right by the hunter now sitting in wait!

Having a buddy drop you off at a field-edge stand can take advantage of this same approach. As with the two bucks discussed at the start of this chapter, deer in farm country become nearly oblivious to trucks and tractors. In areas where hunting from a truck is rare, deer have learned to simply wait for them to pass and then return to their normal routine. When a hunter is dropped off in this manner, it allows him to pass by bedded deer that would turn inside out if the hunter had been walking. Better still, at dark this method can be used to pick up the hunter who has been watching a field, without him having to either wait for the field to clear of feeding deer or blow them out when climbing down from the stand.

A variation of this same approach can be used in areas where foot traffic is common. Parks that allow hunting, many areas of public lands, and even some private acreages receive a lot of use from people birdwatching, walking dogs or simply hiking. Just as deer grow accustomed to farm traffic, those living in such situations learn to simply sit tight, wait for the foot traffic to subside, and then return to their normal activity. Having someone walk with you to your stand, only to leave the way he or she came in, as well as come back to pick you up, serves the same purpose as getting dropped off and retrieved by a vehicle. The deer see this passing person as nothing more than a momentary inconvenience. On the flip side, if they watch a hunter walk through and don't see him return, they know to avoid that area in the near future

Conditioning Deer

For those who wish to go the extra mile, it's possible to condition deer to human activities that help us avoid spooking them as we approach or leave our stands. More and more people are purchasing land for recreation. Although this is often intended for hunting, it also can include providing a place for kids to ride their ATVs, for the family to ride horses, or simply a romantic nature trail to share with your spouse.

When designing this trail system, regardless of what the mode of transportation might be, why not lay it out so it can be used to access the land for hunting? Provided that the recreational traffic is kept strictly to the trail system, the resident deer will swiftly adapt to it. Before long, they'll actually become tolerant of human activity along the trail. Since it's harmless, as well as limited to one corridor, the deer will become conditioned to simply lie low until the people pass and then resume their activities.

Now, if the trail is laid out properly, a hunter can use it until it reaches the point closest to the stand and then cut off to his destination. The end result can be an effective, low-impact way of cutting right through the heart of the deer woods.

As a bonus, you can even pitch your wife on the importance of picking up that hunting — errrrr, I mean recreational — land so that it provides all of you the opportunity to more closely bond as a family. I mean, what would she rather have: her son and daughter playing video games and getting into unthinkable trouble all weekend, or the entire family enjoying rides through God's creation? It's almost child abuse not to buy that land . . . you know, for the good of the family. Sure, as long as you get it you might as well hunt it, but it's really the priceless benefits it provides the little ones that you're most concerned about.

Conclusion

Few other things have the ability to mess up a deer woods faster than poorly planned entrance and exit routes. Before long, an area previously thriving with deer can suddenly seem void of activity. Truth be told, most often the deer are still there; however, that's little consolation when their activity is predominantly nocturnal. Carefully and creatively planning entrance and exit routes goes a long way toward keep a hunting area fresh and the taxidermy bill high. I might have been able to help with explaining the importance of buying land for the family, but I'm afraid you're on your own when justifying why you need another mount in the den.

Problem Prevention

STEVE BARTYLLA

Problem Prevention

**SUCCESS IS ALL
ABOUT AVOIDING
BAD DECISIONS.**

When laying out the flow of this book, I was pleased to see that these last two chapters seemed to fit logically at the end. Although it was not a purposeful act on my part to hold them to this point, it conveniently worked out so that I believe I saved the best for last. It isn't that these final two will be the best written or have the smoothest flow. On the contrary, they'll be choppy, disjointed and blatantly void of hunting stories. Still, they might be the most condensed, information-packed writings on what not to do and how sometimes seemingly little things can make a positive difference in your stand-hunting results. A few topics have been previously mentioned, but even they are important enough to be brought up again.

Previously Covered Topics

It would be wrong of me not to once again hammer home how critical it is to get in and out of stand locations undetected, as well as not leaving tattletale odors behind to betray us. When we don't put in the extra effort to effectively deal with these issues, we not only cripple our current efforts but also educate deer for future hunts.

Setting up right on top of sign or hunting from stands without ample cover also has already been covered. Still, I couldn't do a chapter on common mistakes without mentioning them. Simply picturing a buck walking down the trail and envisioning how the shot would play out can alert you to a bad stand choice. Remember, *seeing* that big buck isn't the ultimate goal — *harvesting* him is. If your stand setup makes that a dicey proposition, find a way to remedy it.

Overhunting

Another factor that ties into educating deer is overhunting the same stand or woodlot. Simply put, if the stand is hunted during the right phase of the season, the first time in is typically the best. Even when we take every precaution we can for selecting routes, cutting odors and minimizing disturbances, it's darn near impossible to not leave any clues behind.

So, the question then becomes: How much pressure is too much? It depends a lot on the phase of the season, whether the hunter's routes are low-impact or not, the stand's ability to conceal the hunter, and the hunter's success rate of not getting winded.

During the rut, because bucks are covering so much ground, I have no problems with hammering the same stand sites hard. Because bucks during this phase are here today and gone tomorrow, with new ones replacing them, I feel this constant reshuffling all but eliminates the need to rotate stand sites. Except, that is, when hunting family group bedding areas. Then I don't feel it's mission critical to remain undetected, but I still believe that keeping the does ignorant has a value. A buck scent-checking from the downwind side of the bedding area may not know that no one's home until it's too late, but if we drive the does out, it eliminates the chance of a buck following a hot doe out of the bedroom.

On the other hand, if I have a funnel stand that's by far my best option, I'll sit it every day. Ideally, I have three or four stands that I can rotate between, in an effort to keep the resident does more ignorant. However, I won't sit a stand that I believe is much inferior to my best option during the rut. For those hunters who have problems with getting winded, that makes it important to either have a stand for each wind direction covering the travel corridor or sit some other locations where the wind works. Sure, the bucks may be filing through from parts unknown, but that doesn't mean that they'll walk through a hunter's odor stream to pose for the shot.

During the early and late phases, if a stand is hot and I can go completely undetected, I'll hunt it until I either harvest the deer or see the first signs of damage. Those signs would include things like a drop in deer sightings or nervous behavior. Upon noting either occurrence, I give the stand at least four days off.

More commonly, when going undetected isn't as easy, I'll rotate stands so that no one site is hunted more than once in any five-day period. Unless educating deer from our hunting efforts becomes routine for a site, that's typically enough of a break to keep the deer at ease. One way or another, we must hunt stands in a manner that keeps our odds favorable and targeted animals ignorant. To not do so makes taking a bruiser a far more challenging endeavor.

Human Odor

The last of the three biggest stand-killing threats is either not playing the wind or not taking extreme odor-reduction steps. Is one more critical than the other?

I've always had several problems with the concept of keeping the wind in my face to save me. First, the wind isn't a constant. Anyone who's ever sat around a barbeque pit or campfire realizes that the wind nearly always shifts directions many times over a few hours, often carrying smoke in every conceivable direction. The same thing happens when we're on stand — even one high in a tree. Because the wind switches directions so frequently, a hunter who relies strictly on the wind to keep him undetected is largely counting on luck. He just hopes that the buck of his dreams walks down the trail when the wind is blowing his odor somewhere else. Where this comparison falls apart is that the smoke around the pit is much more forgiving than our own odor stream. The smoke is significantly hotter than the air that surrounds it, and even on warm and windy days it rises. Our own odors aren't that cooperative, even on cold days.

The next reason I don't like to rely purely on the wind to hide me is that many good stand locations then are automatically disqualified because of swirling winds or the likelihood of deer approaching from the "wrong" direction. The narrow valley torn up with scrapes produces swirling winds that won't allow for hunting the wind, except possibly on a calm morning. The same can be said for that hub of converging deer trails in the middle of the woods. We can easily come up with a dozen other scenarios that are risky at best if we rely strictly on playing the wind.

Furthermore, regardless of how hard we try to pinpoint where deer will travel, they tend to be uncooperative and appear where they aren't expected. When the deer that shows up in the wrong spot happens to be the buck in which

Once you've been picked off by the buck you're after, the game changes — and not in a positive way. Photo by Ron Sinfelt.

we've invested a great deal of scouting and hunting effort, his appearance downwind of the stand can be more than a little disappointing.

What's the solution? For starters, it helps to understand wind flow. When the wind is steadily blowing across perfectly flat terrain, anyone can visualize how a steady breeze flows. However, throw in some terrain breaks and the thermals that come into play around sunrise or sunset, and things get a little harder for many to predict.

The biggest breakthrough for me came when I began to visualize the wind flowing as water does. Anyone who has worked his way up a trout river has seen how flowing water reacts to an obstruction. Water flows over, around or under it, swirling behind any obstacle it encounters. The same holds true for air. That's precisely why a hunter can be walking across a field thinking the north wind is perfect for his stand at the base of the east-west ridge, only to get there and have the wind seem to be coming out of the south. Once you conceptualize wind as flowing water, it's much easier to predict its flow at specific locations.

To further our understanding, we must factor in thermal currents. Simply put, hot air rises and cold air falls. In the morning, the ground is typically warmer than the air. Therefore, just as the smoke from a campfire rises, the air blanketing the ground rises as it's heated from the earth, carrying our odors with it as it travels upwards. With the sun heating the air throughout the day, the earth becomes comparatively cooler. In turn, the earth cools the air closer to its surface, reducing or completely eliminating the rising effect often seen in the morning. Ever notice that you tend to get winded more in the afternoon than in the morning? That's why. In calmer conditions, nature typically helps to protect us from a deer's nose during our morning hunts.

Understanding thermals, as well as how air currents react to structure, allows us to better predict the flow of our odors and select stands accordingly. However, to be truly safe, we must be careful to pick stands with a high probability of deer exclusively moving through on only one side of them. Setting a stand on the outside edge of a funnel is a good example of doing this. Even so, the stand can then be hunted only when the wind is steadily blowing into the area void of deer activity. If it switches, abandoning the stand is often the smartest and safest choice.

The other option for beating a deer's nose is to religiously kill every foreign odor we can. Doing so takes a dedicated approach, but it can be done.

As I'm sure has become obvious by now, I always wear a complete Scent-Lok suit, along with making certain to always wash all of my clothing, shower, and spray down with Scent Killer products, before I head afield. I'm far from alone in that. However, many fellow hunters who take such steps fall short of completing the process of becoming scent-free, because they overlook seemingly little details that can make a big difference.

We must remember that a whitetail couldn't care less if it's winding the hunter, his stand, bow or any other "human" object in the woods. All the deer knows is that its nose has told it something's wrong. To successfully combat this, we must take inventory of every object we carry with us while hunting.

When doing so, my first step is to analyze if I truly need a given item. If I can live without it on the hunt, leaving it at home makes for one less object that can trip me up. For example, I don't really have to carry my wallet to the stand — I can carry just my ID, deer permit and hunting license — but I find a wristwatch and eyeglasses indispensable. So the wallet stays home and my glasses and watch are washed in hydrogen peroxide each time before I head out. Taking it further, I have a watch that I only wear for hunting. Whenever practical, the items that go into the woods with me are used exclusively in the woods and then sealed in a scent-free container when not in use.

Furthermore, all of my equipment must be treated. My bow case has a tight seal. Its inside is washed several times during the season, along with being sprayed down with Scent Killer once a week. At the same time I do this, or any other time I feel they've been contaminated, I wash my bow, arrows and even broadheads with hydrogen peroxide. My deer rifle is oiled using one of several brands that also serve as masking scents. My hunting boots and Elimitrax are washed weekly, both inside and out, with a mixture of Scent Killer soap and water. After drying outdoors, they're ready for use. If it will be a while before their next use, I dump about a cup of baking soda into them and then place them inside a sealed container.

For a bowhunter, what gets sweatier than the wristband of a release? We use them all summer long and when practicing during deer season. All the while, bacteria are thriving and producing noxious odors. Then, when preparing for a bowhunt, we shower, slap on our hunting gear, grab our release, and head into the woods. As the deer snorts and torpedoes the other direction, we curse our scent-eliminating products, never considering that we're wearing a stinky release. That could just as easily be our grunt tube, knife, safety harness, sandwich or any other item we have with us.

The point I'm trying to make is that our efforts and supporting products will only go as far as we let them. To be able to get by the nose of a whitetail, we must treat everything we bring with us accordingly. In the case of my release, I have two identical releases. One is used for practice during the off-season, the other only for practice and hunting once bow season begins. This is done strictly to ensure that it's functioning properly. After that, it's washed once a week, sealed until use, and sprayed down, along with my calls, boots and all accessories outside of my bow, right before heading into the woods.

Another common mistake occurs as a hunter steps out of the shower. He's just thoroughly scrubbed every inch of his body — but what does he do next? He reaches for a towel. It just happens to be the same towel that his mother, wife, girlfriend or he himself washed and dried . . . dried with a scented fabric softener sheet. There he is, rubbing perfume odors all over his glistening skin and dripping hair. As silly as this might sound, you'd be shocked at how many hunters do just that, counteracting the benefit of showering in the first place.

In addition, address your vehicle. Never wear your boots or hunting clothing in a vehicle you're traveling to a hunting location in. I wear treated clothing to my parking location, then shed that clothing and put on fresh underlayers. Also, when I'm depending on it for hunting, I try to clean my truck's interior at least once a week. Even with that, you should remove any air fresheners, lay plastic bags on the seat, and, if possible, keep the windows down as you drive. When I use an ATV, I wear a rainsuit to minimize contamination from foreign odors.

This might seem like a lot of extra work, and it is. However, I have no doubt that I've harvested many more whitetails because of this extra effort. On more than one occasion, I've had a big buck oblivious to my presence, even as my breeze detector fluttered directly toward him. A handful of occurrences in which deer appear to be downwind and remain unaware can be written off as the result of freakish thermals, but when this occurs numerous times each week, over the course of years, your scent-elimination efforts are working.

Breaking The Pattern

Yet another way to help keep stands fresh is by being unpredictable in hunting them. As I hope was illustrated in the earlier chapters, whitetail food sources, behaviors and patterns change throughout the season, so sitting in the same stands over and over throughout the season is rarely productive. Not only does shifting stand-placement strategies help keep us in deer, it also goes a long way toward breaking the predictable patterns we unwittingly tend to fall into. These patterns, such as taking the same route each time in to a stand, hunting the same stands over and over, calling in the same manner every time, and other repetitive actions that eventually educate deer can all be counterproductive.

Of course, there are situations, such as repeatedly using a flawless entry and exit route, in which repetition is advisable. However, it's more often better to shake things up and keep deer off balance. For example, it might not seem like a bad idea to approach a stand by walking through the same valley each time, but what if a really nice buck just happens to be bedding on one of the surrounding ridge fingers? Because the hunter doesn't present immediate danger, the buck does nothing more than watch him walk through. Still, are the odds good that the buck will later follow the hunter to the stand? More often than not, the answer would be no. Now, if the hunter happens to come in every other time from the other side of the ridge, the odds of connecting with that buck go up significantly. And if there happen to be two or more stands — each with its own route — along the buck's various travel corridors, we take our chances up yet another notch.

When bucks have you stumped, reassess your strategy. Maybe you've fallen into a predictable pattern. Photo by Ron Sinfelt.

Simply put, unlike activities such as taking the same thorough odor control steps each time, activities that can be patterned by deer should be done in a sporadic manner. Analyzing the activities we perform as hunters and identifying patterns in our behavior provides us the chance to break those patterns that can educate deer. Thus, we increase our odds for success.

Scent Mishaps

Just as with calling the same way each time, using the same scents every trip out can not only decrease their effectiveness, but also educate deer. Don't get me wrong — I rely heavily on scents. Rarely do I not use some in one way or another. Still, it must be done in a way that doesn't alert the animals to our activities.

For example, let's say our favorite scent happens to be an estrous scent. Using this same scent from opening day to close would be bad on many levels. First, an estrous scent is going to be far more consistently successful near, during and after the rut. During the first two phases of the season, curiosity and, to a lesser extent, food attractant scents produce the best results. During the scraping and chase phase, buck urine and tarsal scents, along with estrous scents, can be most effective. From the chase phase on through the rut, I find estrous scents to be my most productive choice. Finally, for the second rut and post-rut, both food lures and estrous scents can be good. Of course, cover scents can be used throughout all of the season.

Another reason that using the same scent every time out can be detrimental is that repeated exposure to the same scents can reduce their effectiveness. Let's say that we are using a food scent. We place some in our shooting lane, where we want the shot to occur, and then climb up into our stand. Because we know that its effectiveness will be decreased whenever a deer investigates it and leaves empty-handed, we place it on a scent wick and take it out with us when we leave. Still, some of the scent is bound to drip on the ground. An hour after dark, a buck passing downwind alters his course and comes in to the scent to investigate it. Finding nothing, he leaves. A few days later, the entire event is repeated, with our buck again stopping to check our scent. Now, the next time we hunt the stand, the buck happens to be traveling downwind while we are on stand. With him having twice investigated it without finding the resulting food, what are the odds he will come in? Repeatedly using the same scent can reduce its effectiveness on deer previously exposed to it.

Now let's take a little different view. What happens if he does come in that first time and smells us, bolting before he enters shooting range? Then the second time he comes in after we leave, he smells human odor on the branch because we didn't wear rubber gloves while placing our scent. How often does he have to have similar encounters before he associates this odor with danger? Once that happens, our scent serves to drive the animal away, instead of luring him into shooting range.

Any scent or lure, with the exception of those consisting exclusively of the urine of animal species native to the area, can have an alarming effect on deer if they have repeatedly had bad experiences with it. Switching among three or four scents and lures all but eliminates this possibility. Because the urine of animals native to the area is so prevalent in the habitat, scent made exclusively from them also eliminates this possibility.

That is, unless that animal is a deer's natural predator. For that reason, I never use wolf, coyote or fox urine. Of the three, fox urine is by far the most commonly used cover scent. However, having watched deer run from the odor of an approaching fox numerous times, I personally don't recommend using it. I don't know if it's because deer are incapable of differentiating between the various species of canines or if it's due to the rare occurrences of foxes taking newborn fawns. Regardless of why, having videotaped a mature doe fleeing the field with her fawns, only to return to charge the fox away, along with the times they simply bolted at the odor, I can say at the very least that the smell of fox urine makes a percentage of deer very nervous. That's more than enough to convince me to make another selection for a cover scent, most often either straight doe or buck urine.

The full range of curiosity, food, estrous, buck and cover scents all can be used very effectively. It's up to us to see that we do so intelligently, as well.

Checking Stands And Being Safe

A further tragic mistake that many tree stand hunters make is not using safety restraints. Today's safety restraints have become so quiet, comfortable and effective that there's no longer a viable excuse for not wearing one. Personally, I had always hated them because of the limited range, potential for odors, and noise they made. I figured that if I was simply careful I wouldn't have a concern. Well, simply put, I was an idiot. Thankfully, I corrected this foolishness before something tragic happened. Granted, my reasons for disliking safety restraints were valid in early years. Today, I find that I completely forget I even have them on. In other words, there's no longer a reason not to use them, except for stupidity.

The same holds true for wearing them as we hang the stand. Let's face it, sitting in a properly hung stand is much safer than hanging from one arm, 30 feet up a tree, trying desperately to screw that last step into the oak, only to then do your best balancing act when strapping the stand on.

Tree stands that are hung before the season need to be checked carefully before hunting. This

Always check tree stands to be sure they're in perfect condition — but wear a safety restraint anyway. Photo by Ron Sinfelt.

accomplishes two things. First, it could save a life. If a red squirrel decided to chew through the strap, a cable has somehow frayed, or a nut has disappeared, it's much nicer to learn about these pesky issues ourselves, instead of the county sheriff figuring this out after your body has been dragged from the woods.

Either making a midday trip in before you intend to hunt or allowing extra time the first hunting day for inspection purposes gives us a better chance of survival, along with providing the opportunity to fix the issues and still effectively hunt the stand. After the first thorough inspection, for each subsequent hunt a quick safety check should be made of all the potential failure spots on a stand. It only takes a few seconds to look at the strap or chain, glance over the cables, and check the nuts. Those seconds could save your life. These steps are even more important when checking for rotted wood and decaying nails and bolts in permanent tree stands.

Another safety precaution is required when using screw-in tree steps. Steps that have been left in a tree for months or more can cause the wood surrounding them to rot. Because of that, they should be repositioned at least once just before the start of each new hunting season, particularly those in softwood trees. Naturally, the steps themselves should be checked as well.

The last thing you need when a deer is coming in is to have your stand squeak. Treating the stand's moving parts with a few drops of vegetable oil could prevent it from happening to you. Photo courtesy of Steve Bartylla.

Also, regardless of whether you're using screw-ins, ladders, rails, sticks or branches to get up a tree, three out of four of your combination of hands and feet should always be in secure contact with steps. That way, it's harder to lose your balance and slip and less likely for a breaking step to send you tumbling to the ground.

It should go without saying that stands should never be placed in dead or dying trees. Let's face it: hunting already comes with a risk factor. To add an unnecessary risk is foolish.

Tolerating Problems

Another potentially devastating mistake many hunters make is living with known problems. If the stand squeaks when you're shifting your weight, try resetting it tighter on the tree. Trees naturally constrict and expand. Simply resetting it is often enough to rid the stand of noise. If that doesn't cut it, try putting on a new washer or applying vegetable oil to the culprit. If all else fails, get a new stand.

If a branch looms in your shooting window, take it out. If the arrow makes a scratching sound when dragged over the rest, take the time to put moleskin or another sound dampener on the rest. When you notice that a slightly different stand position would be better, move. If the scope keeps fogging up, coat it with an anti-fogging agent. Whatever the issue is, fix it.

No consistently successful trophy hunter I know will live with problems he's capable of fixing. Harvesting trophy bucks requires a high level of time and effort. To risk wasting an opportunity because of tolerating a known problem is a potentially disheartening mistake.

Settling

Similarly, in the vast majority of cases, settling for what you have, be it hunting land or stand locations, is rarely not a mistake. Every hunter has an upper end number of properties and stands he can effectively hunt each year. When inventorying my setups after scouting, I rank them from best to worst. My annual goal is to replace at least my worst hunting spot with a better one. Certainly, there may be properties you want to hunt each season solely for personal reasons. There are even individuals who have a surplus of high quality acreage already at their disposal. Both are in the minority. Furthermore, unless you own the land, one constant in hunting private land is that you always seem to eventually lose it.

In reality, the balance of actual time spent hunting, finding better land, and scouting is about equal for most of the dedicated trophy whitetail hunters. That doesn't mean that everyone must take this approach, but it does put into perspective the importance placed on always striving to find better land and more productive stand locations.

As already alluded to, the same approach to upgrading land should be applied to replacing the stand sites that weren't productive. Unless I have a tangible reason to believe a stand site that didn't at least yield a trophy buck sighting will improve the next season, I do all I can to replace it with a more promising location.

On rare occasions when a setup fails but looks too promising to give up on, I'll give it a second year to produce. Still, that's a rare exception. Simply put, unless something changes, such as an emergence of new mature buck sign, the locating of a favorable new food source, or the maturing to shooter status of a buck passed on the previous year, stands don't tend to get better on their own. Be it stand sites or hunting land, continually replacing the worst of the lot with something better helps ensure that our success rates continue to improve.

Too Much Help

I know that more than a few readers won't care for me classifying this as a common mistake, but all too often, in-season scouting or visiting stand sites with a hunting buddy is just that: a mistake. Sure, when you're covering ground while scouting during the off-season, having another perspective on things can be helpful, but during deer season the cost is just too high in my opinion. It's hard enough to travel through the deer's home and not tip them off when we're by ourselves. Adding other hunters to the equation makes it X times more difficult, with X representing the number of people dragged along in the woods with you.

This is made even worse when those companions don't place the same premium on keeping deer ignorant that you do. Sure, you may have taken every precaution, but if they didn't, your efforts are minimized. It most definitely is nice to have another person along to help carry things, get a second opinion from, trim branches as you hang the stand, and even just to talk to. Still, when pursuing a trophy buck, I believe the trade is seldom worth the price.

Not Sitting Long Enough

If at all possible, when you think it's time to get out of your stand after a morning hunt, sit another hour.

As much as I wish I could take credit for those words, they came from the mouth of my own younger brother, Joe. I've found this approach to be very helpful. Many hunters believe that if the first hour or two of daylight passes without their seeing a buck, the action is over for the morning. During all but the first two phases of the season and the last one, bucks can realistically be moving during any portion of the day. During the first two phases and the last one, I have far better luck during late morning and early afternoon than I ever do the first few hours. Impatience is one of the whitetail hunter's worst enemies.

The Comfort Factor

Another major enemy is being uncomfortable. Few whitetail hunters can remain silent, motionless and alert in an uncomfortable stand. Even fewer are willing to sit as long as they would in one that provided comfort. When your head isn't in the game, it's much easier to blow opportunities. Having comfortable stands is one way to combat that problem.

As bad as uncomfortable stands can be, dressing inappropriately is even worse. There are two approaches I take. In relatively warm weather, I dress lightly going in, have extra layers in my pack, and add another layer in the stand if I get cold.

When temperatures near the freezing point, I've successfully used the layering method. However, I abandoned it once I found The Heater Body Suit. This is an outer shell you put on at the stand. Because of its insulation and the way it contains the body's own heat, the suit provides comfort in temperatures ranging from the high 30s on down into negative numbers.

Although comfort is reason enough to use this product, its overall effectiveness shouldn't be overlooked. Wearing it as a pack to the stand allows me to dress lightly and helps to eliminate the sweat and odors created while getting in. Surprisingly, I've found this very beneficial on days when the temperature is in the 30s. Instead of either getting very sweaty on the way in or creating an odor plume around my stand by changing clothes there, I dress very lightly and regulate my own heat retention by zipping The Heater Body

The Heater Body Suit is one of the author's favorite gear items for cold-weather hunting. You simply slip out of the suit to shoot your bow or gun. Photo by Steve Bartylla.

Suit up and down to achieve the ideal comfort level as I walk.

Once I get into my stand, all I must do is slide on the suit, and I'm ready to deal with rain, sleet, wind and/or cold. As deer approach, the suit easily slips from the upper body and allows for the shot. An easily overlooked advantage is that the lack of layers lets me easily draw the bow or hold the firearm without the risk of my accuracy being affected. Regardless of whether you use one of these suits or take the layered approach, being comfortable will help you fill more tags and make the experience far more enjoyable than the alternative.

Conclusion

When reading this chapter, if you found you were guilty of one or more of these mistakes, don't feel bad. I'm not too proud to admit that I've committed each and every one of them. Again, I've been able to learn far more from my mistakes than from my successes. Each topic could have included a story on how this tripped me up at least once. As hunters, we can't be afraid to make mistakes or expect that we'll never do so. The key is to learn from them and make the necessary corrections, turning negatives into positives.

Details that Matter

TOM INDREBO

Details that Matter

**THE SMALL STUFF
CAN ADD UP TO
SOMETHING BIG.**

As necessary as it might be to relive the agony of past stand-hunting mistakes, as was done in Chapter 14, I want to end this book on a high note. What follows is advice that can lead you to triumph in the deer woods. I've found that some of these tips, such as how to beat buck fever, have been a tremendous help alone. Others might not seem that significant. However, when you add up the "little things," you often get the results you want. I hope that will be the case for you.

Shooting Practice

For my success rate on whitetails to be high, I simply must practice my shooting regularly. This applies to both bow and firearms seasons. I'm constantly amazed at how many hunters shoot their rifle once a year and call it good. If I did that, I'd feel that I was playing with a severe handicap. Be it a firearm or a bow, I want my shooting equipment to feel like an extension of my body. When it does, my shots are so much more natural, relaxed and accurate than they otherwise could be. For me, the only way to accomplish this is through practicing.

Taking it the next step, most of us practice shooting bull's-eyes, but how many of us practice harvesting deer? There's a tremendous difference between shooting a buck in the woods and shooting a target at the firing range or in the back yard. The firearms hunter isn't often provided with a chair, table, sand bag, a lack of obstructions, and all day to take a shot at a stationary buck of a lifetime. Still, that scenario is the only way most ever practice. It's great for zeroing in the scope, but it does almost nothing to prepare anyone for a shot at a trophy whitetail.

Instead, always thinking safety first, spend a few days before the season shooting targets in the woods, in large native grass fields, or in any other location that comes close to the setting in which you'll be hunting. At various distances, practice using shooting sticks, bracing against trees, and shooting freehand. Also,

There are two kinds of target practice: that which sights in the weapon, and that which sights in the shooter. Begin both long before deer season starts. Photo by Ron Sinfelt.

force yourself to rush shots. These activities help hone the skills we'll need for harvesting deer and show us our limitations, as well. Then, as we're walking back to the truck and a big buck pops up 200 yards away, we don't have to waste time wondering if we can make the shot. We already know and are much better prepared to pull it off.

The same holds true for bowhunting. If all we do is shoot at targets in the back yard, how does it help us keep proper tree stand form, estimate yardage, or decide if we can thread the arrow through that softball-sized opening? As with firearms, practicing in the back yard is important for sighting in the bow, but it doesn't necessarily address harvesting animals.

To help yourself achieve proper tree stand form, hang a stand strictly for practicing. Until tree stand form becomes second nature, start each practice session from the stand by pretending the target is horizontal to your position. Then, draw the bow and bend only at the waist until the pin rests on the real target. To incorporate twists and turns into practice sessions, purposefully set your feet in a different directions, draw horizontally, bend your waist to the level of the target and then twist your hips until you're on it. Shooting in every awkward position I can come up with helps my form immensely in the real-world hunting situations we all face.

Improving yardage-estimation skills can be done in numerous ways. When doing routine daily activities, such as walking down a street, pick an object, estimate its distance and then count the paces as you approach. (Of course, this only helps with yardage estimation if you've already determined the length of your stride and can thus convert paces to yards.) Or, while experiencing lulls during hunting, scan the area for deer. When confident that none are present, select an object, estimate its range, and test yourself with a rangefinder. Also, when practicing in the back yard, abandon the yardage marker after getting sighted in. Instead, pick random spots, turn, guess the yardage, and shoot. These easy tasks will all help you hone your yardage-estimation skills considerably.

Another effective bowhunting practice method is stump shooting in the woods. Stalking stumps, as well as small game, not only puts yardage estimation to the test but also helps improve our stalking skills. Whether it's a stump or a squirrel, treating each stalking target as if it were a record-book buck makes pulling it off on the real thing that much easier.

Improving your ability to gauge whether you can thread the needle is relatively easy for those who use sights. The key to threading needles is first finding a hole that lines up with the target. Next, estimate the hole's distance, then the deer's. Place the proper pin on the deer, as if the obstruction weren't present. Then, see where the pin closest to matching the yardage of the obstruction falls. If the obstruction pin is in the opening, and the arrow flies true, the shot is doable.

For example, let's say a deer is 30 yards away, with only a softball-sized opening to his vitals. With the distance to the obstruction being about 20 yards away, settle your 30-yard pin on the deer's vitals. Next, see where the 20-yard pin falls in the opening. If it lines up with the hole, and the shot is true, the arrow should hit its mark. If not, the shot shouldn't be taken. With a little practice conducted by purposefully setting targets so that they're partially obstructed, threading the needle can become relatively easy.

Beating Buck Fever

To further help my archery practice, but even more so to help me beat buck fever, I strive to make all shooting practice as realistic as possible. To do this, I slap on my camo, grab a McKenzie 3-D deer target and head for a practice stand in the woods. This setting, along with the realism of McKenzie targets, makes such practice as close to the real thing as it gets. This is especially true when you schedule the trip for the last 30 minutes of daylight. As a side bonus, doing so helps prepare us for the low-light situations we often face while hunting.

To add the final touch of realism, I mentally picture the deer approaching. I then select the time to draw, hold at full draw for some time (as if having to wait for the buck to give me a good shot), and then let my arrow fly. This not only exposes me to all of the elements of hunting, but it also helps me keep calm when the true money shot occurs. Each time I draw on a deer, I tell myself that I'm merely practicing. As silly as that sounds, it really does help me stay calm. After all, I tell myself, I've shot countless arrows from tree stands at deer in the woods. The only difference is that this one will run away and fall over after the shot.

Most often, buck fever comes from a lack of confidence in making the shot. When you prepare the best you can and play the mind games of pretending that your practice is the real thing, it becomes harder to believe you'll blow it on a deer. In turn, the cases of nerves get less severe each time.

Chasing Other Prey

This is also why I try to take advantage of any off-season hunts for other species. Any animal, be it large or small, presents the opportunity to sharpen our hunting skills. For example, even for grizzled veterans of the stand, sitting in a tree and watching bears pile into the bait can be a valuable testing ground. You can test your odor-control techniques and your ability to place and conceal your stands. You must choose when to move and draw. You must learn to remain calm during the shot.

If you increase your confidence to the point that you truly believe you'll take that buck of a lifetime, your odds of doing it are much better. When you can remain calm and pull off a successful shot on a 300-pound black bear, chances are good that you can do it on a deer, too. The more species and hunting situations we put ourselves in, the better prepared we are to drag that buck from the woods.

Practicing While Hunting

At first, it might surprise you that I believe practice shouldn't end when you climb into a deer stand. One of the first things I do after getting settled in is to practice drawing my bow or aiming my firearm. With my weapon in whatever position I anticipate it being in while hunting (for me, that's typically in my hand), I visualize the most common approaches a buck would take and go through my preparation for the shot.

This serves several useful purposes. First, by doing such things as shifting, picking spots the animal would be when I react, and aiming, it helps mentally prepare me for any probable scenario that might unfold. Having already run through it before an animal approaches on that route, I already know how I will react and am better prepared for the shot.

Of course, things do occasionally deviate from the mind's vision, so we must remain flexible. Still, even when nothing goes as planned, this practice is beneficial. Any mental preparations help us to remain calmer in crunch time. Furthermore, these acts can alert us to all sorts of potential problems. If a branch with dried leaves is likely to be hit when raising your bow, you need to know it before a deer appears. Same thing if the stand squeaks when you move toward the end for a certain angle of shot. It's so much nicer to know about these things before a 180-inch buck passes 15 yards from your tree. With knowledge of problems, we have the ability to fix them or compensate for them. Conversely, when they catch us by surprise, we most often have the memory of another tail waving goodbye.

Harvesting Bucks In The Spring

Although this was previously mentioned in passing, it's worth repeating that there's no better time to scout for the lull, scraping, chase and rut phases of deer season than before leaf-out occurs. With all of the previous year's rubs and scrapes so plainly visible, it's so much easier to identify travel patterns, follow rub lines to a buck's bedding area, locate heavily used funnels, pinpoint which family group's bedding areas inspired the most rut sign, and locate those heavily used primary scrapes. Most years, my success is tied tightly to the results of my spring scouting efforts.

This is also the time when the majority of my stands are hung for those four phases of the season. With the exception of the lull phase, the others are timed in most areas to occur after the leaves drop. A stand hung in a tree decorated with leaves looks completely different once the tree is bare. A ground blind site prepped in September often stands out like a sore thumb in November. In the Northern areas I most often hunt, many stands that look very well concealed in mid-summer through mid-October are simply unhuntable once late October rolls around. The only way to overcome this problem is to add natural or artificial cover to them.

Selecting and preparing stand sites before the leaves appear in the spring provides a chance to gauge the conditions and helps ensure that we won't be in for unpleasant surprises when crunch time rolls around. As mentioned earlier in the book, it also allows us to make disturbances that are long since forgotten by deer by the time the season hits. The freshest, most productive stands I sit are almost always the ones I prepped in the spring.

Creating Funnels

Yet another productive spring activity is creating funnels. Many areas don't have well-defined funnels. Instead of cursing your luck and living with it, if you either own the land or can get permission from its owner, you can take steps toward making your own funnels.

The easiest way is by creating fence crossings. In areas which have fence lines that deer must work a little to cross, select a crossing point or two that are well suited for hunting. Next, invest a little time in discouraging deer from using the other crossing points. To do that, clog the other locations where deer are crawling under and fix up the places where the fence's top is broken or drooping.

With that done, focus on making the crossings by your stands even better. For barbed-wire fences, simply wrapping a strand of wire around the fence and cinching it tight creates both a low spot for deer to jump and an easier path to crawl under. Shoveling out some dirt underneath the fence is the icing on the cake. For other forms of fencing, a little creativity can typically show you how to lower the top a smidge. (Again, however, none of this should be done without permission of the landowner.)

When you're hunting trails leading to fields, piling debris on routes not suited for hunting will help to discourage deer from using them. To further encourage the use of yours, rake about 20 yards clear of grass and debris from the field edge back into the woods. The final result provides the illusion that our trails are the field's only primary entrance and exit routes. Just as importantly, they appear to be the easiest and most popular routes for deer to follow.

To go a step beyond, dropping a large limb or two where the trail splits before hitting your stand also encourages deer to continue on your way. The two keys for greatest success are that both trails should lead to the same general destination and that the obstruction should be placed right at the split, not allowing a deer to take a step or two down the wrong path before encountering it.

To further funnel deer, the trails themselves can be improved. Following the trail and trimming any obstacle that lies in a deer's path — including small branches — makes for easier travel and provides the illusion of heavy usage. When doing this, I create a 3-foot-wide, 6-foot-high "tunnel" that's completely free of even the smallest obstruction. When doing this, it's important to not make the trail wider, or the deer begin to feel exposed. Because they do feel safe, the thicker and nastier the cover, the better the results of this trail clearing can be.

It doesn't take much to get white-tails to cross a fence at a specific point. However, always check with the landowner before altering a fence or other structure. Photos by Steve Bartylla.

None of these methods create the hard funnels that can be found in nature. What they do is offer easier travel, thus encouraging increased deer traffic through certain travel corridors. Often, that's enough to significantly improve a stand site.

A more radical and expensive approach is to erect a section of snow fence or chicken wire solely for the purpose of forcing deer to go around the obstruction. Although I seldom use this method, it's very effective in narrowing the travels of deer through existing funnels that are otherwise too wide for your weapon's effective range.

There are many more ways to help funnel deer. For example, in areas with deep snow, something as simple as pulling a weighted sled down a trail will result in immediate use by local whitetails. The point of this section was to inspire creative thinking. Just because an area's deer movement patterns aren't set up ideally, it doesn't mean you can't make it so they are much better for hunting. It's amazing what a little creative thought and elbow grease can produce.

Theft-Proofing Your Stands

An all-too-frequent reality in many areas is that leaving portable tree stands, ladder stands and even tripods in the woods can result in their theft. The same can be said of popup blinds, but most of these are now so easy to put up and take down that they're rarely left in the field.

Luckily, steps can be taken to greatly minimize the risks of theft. One that works well with strap or chain-on tree stands is to simply remove the screw-in steps, climbing sticks or rails used to climb the tree. Doing that alone effectively eliminates most opportunity theft. If someone really wants the stand, he either has to be carrying a climbing device or return with one. (Fortunately, most stand thieves are lazy.) When I return to hunt, all I must do is put the steps back in place. If screw-in steps were used, I place twigs in the holes they make in the tree, so they're easier to find in the dark.

Another prevention method is chaining the stand to the tree. When using a tripod stand, this requires placing it so that a leg touches a sturdy tree. Although that's not always possible, chaining the other forms of stands to trees is always an option. When doing this, always use a heavy-duty chain that can't be cut with standard bolt cutters. Of course, that effort is wasted if not paired with use of a sturdy padlock. Picking up 6-packs that all open with the same key helps to minimize the confusion of which key goes to which lock. Still, I scratch a letter into each key and lock to be able to easily match them up. Obviously, keeping a spare key in a secure location helps to reduce the chance of a lost key causing us to outsmart ourselves. Between taking these two precautions, I've never lost a single stand.

Harnessing The Power Of Maps

Switching gears back to locating stands, I'd be hard pressed to come up with another tool that's as beneficial as aerial photos or contour (topographical) maps. Learning to read them can help in so many ways that it's a subject worth a book of its own. Because of that, I have no delusions of teaching the reader all there is to know on the subject. The goal of this brief section is simply to provide enough information to be able to get you started.

For aerials, the best advice I can give is to get a relatively low-altitude shot of your property and carry it with you while you scout. By tracking your position on the photo as you move about the property, you'll be able to identify how various features, such as farm fields, native grass fields, thickets, mature woods, deciduous versus coniferous trees, water features, sharp ridges and so on all appear on the photo. With that knowledge, you can then begin to find potential bedding areas, food sources, watering holes, funnels and travel corridors, all without stepping into the woods. Furthermore, plotting the sign found on clear film overlays registered to the photo helps tremendously when you're trying to see the overall movement patterns and for selecting the best stand locations, as well as routes to and from a given stand.

Map reading is a little trickier, but tracking your position while scouting will also help speed the process. This is particularly true when you understand the following concepts.

On most contour maps, wooded areas are shaded green, open areas are white, and water is blue. That alone can help us find potential funnels. (Of course, wooded areas might have been cleared and open areas might have grown into woods since the map was printed, but at least we have a starting point for our scouting.)

Next, the contours provide the ability to visualize relief. Each contour line on a map indicates a line of constant elevation above sea level, often printed in black or brown. The distance in elevation between lines is commonly 20 feet. In that case, the contours divisible by 100 are called index contours. They're represented by thicker lines and are labeled with an elevation. For example, if the 1,300-foot index contour is running along the side of a hill, the next contour going up the hill is the 1,320-foot line; the next one on the downhill side of the index contour shows an elevation of 1,280 feet.

Because contour lines connect areas of the same elevation and are at set intervals, they indicate how flat or steep the terrain is. When contours are spaced relatively far apart, the terrain is fairly flat; the closer together they are, the steeper

If you combine your observations of deer activity with the study of maps and aerial photos, your knowledge of the herd and land will increase rapidly. Photo by Ron Sinfelt.

the terrain. With this understanding, we can begin to see topographical features emerge. These contours allow us to identify ridges, saddles, benches, cuts and more. With that knowledge, we can see how deer most easily travel through an area, along with locating topographical features.

While carrying a contour map on scouting trips, if you come across a ridge, pull out the map and see what it looks like. If you do the same when you reach a flat, cut, saddle or bench, you'll quickly see how reading the map can help you identify these features.

Such knowledge, paired with a good photo, gives you the ability to do some pretty effective scouting before you even enter the woods. It also will help you find many funnels that otherwise would require blindly stumbling across them while foot scouting. This is a real advantage at any time, but it can be of extreme help for low-impact in-season scouting of a new property.

Clearing Deer

Finally, wrapping up on the topic of one of the themes of this book, here's a tip on keeping deer ignorant of your presence. Any of us who spend a lot of time in stands realizes that there will be occasions when we need to leave but deer just refuse to vacate the surrounding area. As has been illustrated numerous times in this book, allowing any deer to peg you or your stand location is never productive for the long-term success of that stand site or hunting area in general.

So, what do we do when they refuse to leave and we have to get out of there? When either waiting for the deer to eventually move on isn't practical or there appears to be no end in sight, we're forced to allow them to spot us climbing down from the stand. Actually, no, we aren't. Instead, I choose to either snort like a deer or bark like a dog. On occasion, it's taken doing both to get some of the more stubborn deer to leave.

Does it scare them? Well, it does enough to get them to leave. However, snorting deer and barking dogs are relatively common in the woods. If snorts or barks were enough to get them to alter their patterns, they'd be shifting weekly — if not daily. The key is that the deer still have no idea that a human was there. And that, my friend, is a huge key to consistently successful stand-hunting.

Conclusion

It's my sincere hope that this chapter, as well as the rest of the book, provided some nuggets of information that will help you take your buck of a lifetime. I've done my best to relay the information that I feel is most important for stand-hunting success. In its simplest form, this success really boils down to finding the right spot in habitat rich with trophy bucks, hunting the stands intelligently, putting in the time, and being proficient enough with your weapon to make the shot when it's presented.